THE
Archive Photographs
SERIES

CLAY CROSS
COMMUNITY AND COMPANY

The Smith family, local newsagents, gathered outside their home in Cellar Row. They were agents for the *Sheffield Evening Star*, *The People*, the *Derbyshire Times* and the *Derbyshire Courier*. Clay Cross also had its own weekly newspaper, the *Clay Cross Chronicle*, that commenced in March 1900. The editor was Joseph Spriggs and the proprietors were F. Willman and Webster. They did not have the circulation or technology of their competitors and ceased production in December 1910. White's Directory of 1872 lists four newsagents in the town – Thomas Ball, John Cresswell, Maria Edge and Joseph Holmes.

THE
Archive Photographs
SERIES

CLAY CROSS
COMMUNITY AND COMPANY

Compiled by
Cliff Williams

CHALFORD

The Chalford Publishing Company
St Mary's Mill, Chalford,
Stroud, Gloucestershire, GL6 8NX

ISBN 0 7524 1021 0

Typesetting and origination by
The Chalford Publishing Company
Printed in Great Britain by
Redwood Books, Trowbridge

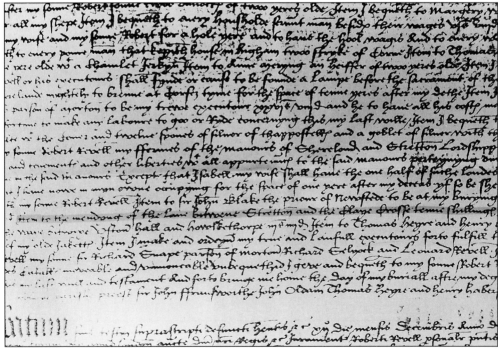

An abstract from John Revill's will of Shirland, dated 28 October 1538, which is the earliest documentary evidence that refers to Clay Cross. The shaded area about two thirds of the way down reads 'Item to the mendeng of the lane betwene Stretton and the Claye Crosse tenne shillings'. This is a most interesting will and makes reference to Revill's lead mining interests; during the sixteenth century lead and iron were smelted in the Stretton furnace.

Contents

Acknowledgements

Once again many thanks to Alan Harris for his help, interest and support with this second volume and particularly with the chapter on the Clay Cross Company. Equally to the Biwater Company for giving me access to their archive and allowing me to reproduce a number of photographs and documents that have made a substantial contribution to our town's history. Thanks again to Dick Childs who over the years has shown a keen and supportive interest in my work and research, even after his retirement from the company.

Sincere thanks to the late Michael Richard Hale, whose photographic knowledge and skills have enhanced several old photographs included in this volume. Thanks to D.P. Sparks for advice and information about Marshall's old motorbikes and also to Glenn Cave, to Geoff and Graham Marshall for interesting details about their family business, to Tony Lomas and Frank Holmes for their assistance in chapter seven and also to Kenning Car and Van Rental, Phillip Griffiths, Sam Thorpe, Warwick Cornford, Eric Trueman, and the late Leslie Spriggs.

Sincere thanks to the following who have in some small way contributed to this volume by either loaning a photograph or supplying information: Mrs King (Tupton), Hannah Churms, Wilf Hallows, Louie and John Rees, Doreen Bowler, Roy Cannon, Arnold Wheatcroft, Colin Bacon, Christine Morgan, Margaret North, Ruth Willet, Bill Tooley, Joe Walton, Ray Pringle, Ernest Whitworth, Cliff Hoben, Dr David Edwards, the late Arnie Lange and Mervin Platts.

Special thanks to Mr M.Williams (Holmgate) for the 1970s 'demolition' photographs; to Mr Charles F. Mason for permission to reproduce his 1835 map of the town; all the staff in the local studies section at the Chesterfield Library and the County Records Office; to the *Derbyshire Times* whose past editions from 1854 are an invaluable source for the study of the town's history – equally the *Derbyshire Courier*, *Derby Telegraph* and the *Clay Cross Chronicle* – and also to the North Wingfield History Group for their interest and support in this project .

Many thanks to the Chalford Publishing Company in deciding to publish this second volume. Finally, 'mega' thanks to my wife and two daughters Anne-Marie and Rachel for their patience and good humour during the time it has taken to research and complete this book – also to Olivia Parker who slept through it all.

If I have excluded anyone in these acknowledgements please accept my sincere apologies.

Introduction

Clay Cross and the Clay Cross Company, the first volume featuring Clay Cross in The *Archive Photographs* Series, emphasised the industrial activities of the company that included some unique images of coalmining, limeworks, coke ovens, proprietors and the like that transformed the village into a dynamic industrial town. It also provided images of the company's paternal structures such as schools, chapels, churches, and houses that helped to recruit, retain and control labour in a highly competitive market.

This second volume depicts and emphasises the town's urbanisation, its social and cultural developments, including many images of busy street scenes and small businesses. Some recently acquired photographs also show the demolition of some of the town's early speculator developments in New Street, Cross Street and Thanet Street, that were built around the 1850s during north-east Derbyshire's boom period. Should a third volume be completed, a unique visual record of nineteenth century housing and buildings of Clay Cross will have been preserved for posterity. The cameras also need to be ready for the imminent changes that will soon obliterate the No. 1 Pit landscape and the Palace cinema.

Included in this volume is a chapter featuring the community, that depicts carnivals, Whit Walks, cinemas, events and activities which are still vivid in many people's memories that will hopefully prompt considerable interest and discussion; perhaps some more visual 'gems' will be uncovered. A chapter on the CXC provides a special record of the company's coal mining activities captured in their unique CXC Gold Medal Coal series. The last section in this book, Politics and Trades Unions, although limited by the space available, could be developed with some evocative images in a further volume which could include sections devoted to those in uniform, transport, sports and recreation. In this respect I would like to make another appeal to readers for any visual and documentary material (it does not have to be particularly 'ancient'), that they think might be useful.

Many thanks are due to all those people and institutions who purchased my previous volume, *Clay Cross and the Clay Cross Company* and particular thanks to those who contributed further information and more photographs that have enhanced this second volume, and which will undoubtably enrich an additional volume. Again, because of deadlines, time restraints and the elusiveness of facts and 'memory blocks' there are alway gaps in productions of this nature – so if any reader has any more information or spots a 'mistake', please let me know so that it can be corrected for the record. In my last introduction I suggested that a more comprehensive written history of the town was in the making and hopefully, the first volume of that history might appear before too long.

I apologise to those people and their families that I inadvertantly misidentified on three photographs in the previous volume. On page 36, the CXC's largest ever vertical casting Bernard Frost should read Bernard Hoben. On page 45, eighty four inch special casting, Cliff Salt should read Oswald Bainbridge, George Newbold should read Thomas Whitworth and the person kneeling is Robert Tidman. Finally, on page 48, re. the pattern shop, Oliver Reed (Freudian slip?) should read Oliver Holmes.

Once again, the Chalford Publishing Company are to be congratulated on deciding to publish this volume in The *Archive Photographs* Series. I am sure that the book's emphasis on the community will appeal to many of the town's indigenous population, as well as providing some context and background for family historians whose ancestors worked and played in Clay Cross

Cliff William
March 199?

This stone, now situated in the churchyard, is reputed to be the base of the cross that once stood at the centre of the crossroads at the top of Clay Lane. In November 1925, George Griffin, a local antiquarian, arranged for this stone to be placed in the churchyard to preserve it for posterity. The plinth on which the base is mounted was brought from Amber Lane Quarry Ashover, and paid for by G.M. Jackson of the Clay Cross Company (CXC). George Kenning of the Kenning Motor Car Company provided the transport free.

One
High Street

Clay Cross crossroads, *c.* 1891, showing a small, single storey cottage attached to the George and Dragon pub. Resident here at this time was Thomas Scott, a coal miner; with his wife Sarah and their children they had been resident in Clay Cross since about 1871. Situated on the right is the New Buck Inn that was opened in July 1876, which replaced the Old Buck Inn. The first landlord of the New Buck was Mr Cook of Dronfield and the photograph was taken by Joseph Buxton, photographer and landlord of the George and Dragon. Next door to the George and Dragon was Arthur H. Cornford, hosier and haberdasher, who came from Torquay. Next door to Cornford's was Robert Lloyd, a chemist and druggist from Nottinghamshire.

A view from Stretton, c.1900, showing the old Turnpike Road side gate on the left that was erected in 1837 to capitalise on the business generated by the tunnelling operations. Standing on the wall to the right is a large, fashioned stone which bears a remarkable resemblance to the reputed base of the cross referred to on page 8. According to Griffin (see page 8), he salvaged it from this particular area and it is indicated on the 1841 tithe map.

A view of Elliott's Yard looking from the Shoulder of Mutton on Stretton Hill side. To the left of the 30 mph sign was the 'short cut' leading to Thanet Street. This path was known as the 'Sheepwalk'. Leading to Longmate's slaughter house, it passed a little, cramped enclosure that is marked on the 1841 town map as the township's pinfold. This was the ancient Stretton manorial pinfold where stray cattle were impounded; it was managed by the 'Pinder' appointed by the manorial court that once sat at Henmill Farm, Holmgate.

A self portrait of Joseph Buxton, landlord of the George and Dragon, who hailed from South Normanton in Derbyshire. His wife, Sarah Anne, was born in Newark and they had seven girls – Minnie, Emily, Florence Louise, Bertha, Francis Alice, Hilda Annie and Sybil Mary. Their servant and pianist in 1891 was Sarah Ann Dobrey from Liverpool.

This photograph of the George and Dragon was also taken by Joseph Buxton, c. 1890. It was probably opened as a pub around 1755 in anticipation of the traffic that was to be generated by the turnpike road opened in about 1757. The names of the landlords are somewhat elusive and the first licensee appears to be Hannah Cutts, whose surety was put up by Benjamin Rooth, malster, in 1755. The Brunt family appear to have purchased the pub sometime later and William Brunt is recorded as being there in 1781.

Whit Walk, *c.* 1954, passing the Buck Hotel, which was demolished in November 1962 by E Ambrose to facilitate better and safer traffic movement. An early reference to the Old Buck Inr appears in the *Derbyshire Courier* in December 1789, when 'Robert Coupe of the sign of the Buck' gave notice that if his wife Mary Coupe 'contracts any debts, or takes up any goods in my name I shall not be accountable for the same after this Day 7th of December 1789'.

A view from the Stretton Road showing the Shoulder of Mutton and Angel Inn and looking north to Chesterfield. Note the thatched roof of the cottage immediately next to the Shoulder and the CXC gas lamp. In November 1934, the Ministry of Transport approved the installation of traffic lights at Clay Cross crossroads to help improve road safety. The buildings at the top of Clay Lane, including the small building attached to the Dragon pub and the one on the High Street, were demolished around 1962.

A front view of the Angel Inn, c. 1956. This pub was also built in the mid-eighteenth century and was a very popular institution throughout the nineteenth century, particularly with the variety of events the various landlords promoted on the Angel Inn running grounds. The landlord in 1836 was Francis Tipping who, on 6 May 1836, was duly appointed keeper of the club box and under-treasurer of the Friendly Society that met there. Annis Hill was landlady in 1848, William Blanksby and John Gill the landlords in 1860 and 1870 respectively.

An advert for the lease of a public house at Clay Cross in 1782, in the occupation of Henry Pemble. This pub with a stable attached was probably the Angel Inn.

The demolition of the Angel Inn, c. 1962, showing the old Friendly Society clubroom. In 1839 the George Stephenson's Favourite Lodge was inaugurated at this pub and to attract customers and increase the lodge's membership, the landlord added this purpose-built clubroom in about 1842. The Angel clubroom was also the headquarters of the Clay Cross No.1 Lodge of the Derbyshire Miners' Association.

Another view of the demolition work. In 1843 George Stephenson actually dined with the members of the Friendly Society at the Angel and a portrait of him was hung in the clubroom. Two other lodges named after the Clay Cross Company proprietors were the Peto and Walmsley Lodge and Sir William Jackson's Favourite Lodge established for their Morton workers in 1870.

The Shoulder of Mutton, September 1994. The history of this beerhouse is difficult to trace and the census returns, together with the directories, do not generally list names of all the beerhouses. An early reference to the pub appears in 1839 when some railway navvies removed the pub sign. The 1881 census refers to a beerhouse on Stretton Road and written in the margin is 'beerhouse no sign'. At this date Thomas Slater and his wife Elizabeth kept the pub which was recorded as the Shoulder and Mutton in the census of 1891.

Cellar Row, c. 1930. This particular row of twenty-two cottages, together with one acre and twenty-eight perches of land was conveyed, in November 1899, to G.M. Jackson in consideration of the natural love and affection of the owners, William Jackson and Thomas Hughes Jackson, for the purpose of qualifying G.M. Jackson as a Justice of the Peace for the County of Derby. This property was to be reconveyed to the owners at any time on demand and with all the accrued rents being paid to them.

Pursgloves and Smarts' butchers situated immediately next to Cellar Row. The three storey building was built around 1868 and occupied by John Herbert Shardlow, butcher and farmer, who was still resident there in 1891. Pursglove's shop was built in about 1878 and in 1891, it was a grocers shop occupied by Abel Beer, from Axminister, Devon. At the end of the First World War is was a derelict beer club, in very bad repair, and was taken over by Mr A. Pursglove who coined the slogan 'The Store of Smiling Service'.

Victoria Buildings and East Tunnel Row. The Victoria Hotel was built for about £4,000 and officially opened on 11 January 1878. Henry Farnsworth purchased the Victoria Hotel from the executors of Abraham Linicare for £3,000 who sold it to a Derby brewery in 1897, for £9,250. In May 1897 the licence was transferred from Henry Farnsworth to William Wilkinson. Aerated Waters moved into this row in 1878, just after the original partnership between Edward Hodgkinson, Joseph Dickenson and John Webb was dissolved in March 1877.

This postcard was posted at Danesmoor on 2 July 1914 to Mr Lewis Fretwell at the old Derbyshire Miners' Convalescent Home, Grosvener Road, Skegness. The new home was not built until 1928. The two gentlemen on the left are the Salway brothers of Hepthorn Lane, who ran a drapery and clothier business at Hepthorn Lane and Grassmoor and who were involved in local politics for a considerable time, particularly with the Clay Lane Board School.

Woolworths, c. 1974. F.W. Woolworth's company obtained planning permission on 26 April 1954 to convert A. Bennett's, 83 High Street, into a multiple store. Arthur Bennett's family were trading in Clay Cross as 'outfitters' from at least the early 1920s. The shop was taken over by Chesterfield Co-operative in August 1974 and after twenty-two years it became the Nice Price store, officially opened on 5 November 1996.

Clay Cross postmen, c. 1925. From left to right: Mr Protheroe, Mr Buckland and Bill Boreman looking up from Holmgate towards Worboys' shop on the High Street. The first 'post' recorded for Clay Cross in 1841, was Henry Pearson, Chapel Street – which was then High Street. The following year George Wood, toll collector, was appointed as the 'post' and in 1846 he was presented with a silver snuff box 'as a token of regard for his character as a trustworthy man'.

Again outside the post office on High Street, c. 1925. From left to right: Mr Protheroe, Mr Myatt, Mr -?-, Mr Fredrick Roe (postmaster), Mr Buckland and Bill Boreman. In 1851 George Wood was still the postmaster with the post office now in Market Street (Stoppards Row); in 1861 he was recorded as the postman and E. Evans was the postmaster. In 1871 Emily Edge and her sister Maria were running the post office, having recently migrated to Clay Cross from Hastings.

Clay Cross Post Office, c. 1930. Emily Edge married Chas Pearson who became postmaster in 1881 and by 1888, Miss Maria Edge (Emily's sister) was postmistress. From 1895 to 1912 Emily Pearson was back in charge. After Emily's retirement Fredrick Roe took over until he retired in 1937 and his wife (Miss B. Cordin), succeeded him until 1964 when she was followed in succession by her daughter Kitty and Jack Wood and then Dennis Macey in 1978.

High Street from the north showing Dawes' shop cornering Eldon Street to the left and the Star Inn situated at the top of Holmgate. This pub was built in about 1857 and the first landlord appears to have been Joseph Marriott, a victualler and farmer of ten acres. The town's LVA was founded there in 1880, and Marriott was one of the founding fathers. Behind the cyclist on the right is Slater and Slaters' shop and the two shops cornering Holmgate were Drabble's drapery shops, built by Mr J. Unwin in 1871.

In May 1964 the Star Inn's license was not renewed but referred to the Derbyshire Compensation Authority for consideration of loss of license. Police Sergeant F. Rundle reported that the Star Inn was owned by Ind Coope (North East) and situated in the area of the town centre where houses were being demolished and people rehoused elsewhere. There were six other public houses within a quarter mile radius and the maximum number of people in the pub at the busiest time of the evening on seven visits was six.

In February 1970 the Ministry of Housing confirmed the purchase order of the Star by the Urban District Council but later substituted the Derbyshire County Council as the purchasing authority. In October 1970 Ind Coope were informed that road improvements involving Holmgate Junction and the A61 were about to commence.

Lester's fruit and vegetable shop on the High Street which, in 1891, was the post office of which Maria Edge was the postmistress. The adjoining three storey building was occupied by John Prestwood Udall, clothier and draper, whose family had occupied the shop since 1857. Joseph Lester first established his family business in the Albert Buildings in 1895: 'Flowers are our business – We grow them for your pleasure'. Prior to this Joseph was an assurance agent and grocer in Cross Street.

A view of the Top Long Row prior to demolition by Martin Cowley in January 1961, when the houses were demolished in rotation from Nos 74 to 31. Incredibly, they had retained their original numbers since 1840, after being built by George Stephenson. These house numbers followed on from the thirty houses that comprised the East and West Tunnel Rows built by the Midland Railway Company. The Bottom Long Row was demolished in February 1960.

This postcard was posted at Clay Cross on 19 September 1908. The Crown Inn, sometimes referred to as the Rose and Crown, was originally built as a farmhouse around 1830. In 1841 it was recorded as a grocers shop and beerhouse, of which George Ellis was the landlord. In 1851 his wife Elizabeth was the innkeeper and farmer of nine acres. She was followed by Richard Woodward in 1857, John Froggatt in 1870, Edward Armstrong in 1891, then a Mr Wood and, in March 1903, Harry Claytor took over.

In 1921 Alfred Webster took over the Crown Inn and was succeeded by his son-in-law Charlie Wakelin in 1953, who was followed by Harvey Knapper, the pub's last landlord. In March 1961 the Brampton Brewery proposed selling the Crown Inn so Clay Cross UDC decided to negotiate a price for the property which would be demolished for road improvements. In June and September 1970, the UDC offered Harvey Knapper alternative accommodation so they could proceed with the demolition.

Two
Market Street

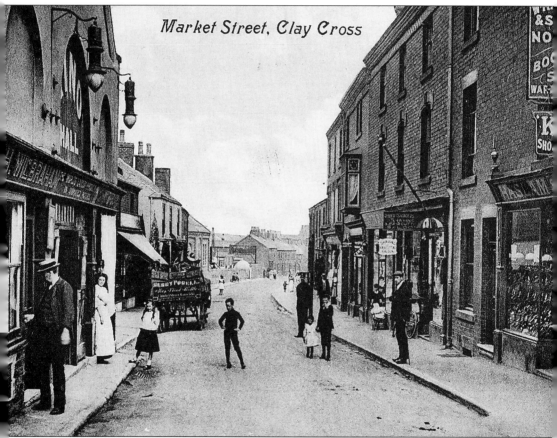

Market Street, *c.* 1912 with the Kino Hall on the left showing butcher John Henry Wilbraham outside his shop front; meat orders could be picked up after the show. The horse and cart waiting outside the Gardener's Inn belongs to Henry Powell. Below Haslam's shoe shop was the shaving and hairdressing salon of Joseph Sanderson, whose family business commenced in Clay Cross around 1850. The Wilbraham family were well established in Clay Cross from about the beginning of the nineteenth century and are recorded in the 1841 census returns. Mr John Henry Wilbraham died on 11 May 1922.

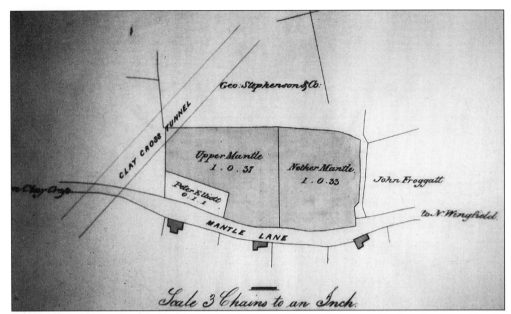

A plan from George Stephenson's property book, *c.* 1840, referring to Market Street as Mantle Lane and named after the two field names, Upper and Nether Mantle. Another plan for 1835 records this 'road' as Church Lane and later Wingfield Lane. The buildings shown on Stephenson's plan are, from left to right, the New Inn, built by Paul Wilbraham in about 1835, the Miner's Arms, built in about 1838 and now known as the Nags Head, but sadly there are no details of the other building shown.

Taylor's Corn Stores, *c.* 1960. This building was a purpose built coffee house opened in April 1879 by J.P. Jackson, manager of the CXC, with the intention 'that such a place as the one they were opening would fill a want long felt in Clay Cross and he hoped it would be well patronised'. The promoters of this scheme were from Sheffield and called themselves the Clay Cross Coffee Tavern Company. The Clay Cross Temperance Movement were also present at the opening.

This postcard was sent from Clay Cross on 2 December 1908, to Miss Adams, Pennine Edge, Duffield, Derbyshire. Sedgwick's Variety Hall at the New Inn was called after its landlord Albert Sedgwick who succeeded Harry Scarlett in about 1905. In 1871, William Scarlet was lodging here and gave his ocupation as billiard marker. The next shop on the right was Worboys' hygenic steam-bakery.

This site was cleared in 1963 as part of the town redevelopment and slum clearance plan that was initially conceived in the mid-fifties. This was the site of Stoppard's Row and Bircumshaw's Houses that made up part of Waterloo Street. The gable end of Park Row can just be seen behind the the fire service training tower and was included in the clearance plan.

in the workhouse,

PROPERTY SALE AT CLAY CROSS.—Last Tuesday evening, at the Star Hotel, Clay Cross, the unsold property in Clay Cross owned by the late Mr. George Froggatt was submitted by Mr. W. D. Botham, of Chesterfield. The property was divided into 15 lots. Lot 1 consisted of 18 dwelling-houses in Market street, Clay Cross, with an off beer license to one of them, with a gross rental of £163 3s. per year. The only bid was £1,400, and it was withdrawn. Lot 2, nine dwelling-houses, also in Market street, standing upon 2,204 square yards, gross rental £96 2s., was sold to Mr. Thomas Houldsworth, Clay Cross, for £1,150. Lot 3, 1,662 yards building land adjoining, was not offered. Lot 4, a villa residence in Market street, standing on 2,410 square yards of land and let at the rental of £30 16s. per year, and containing front and back gardens, and known as "Park Villa," with drawing and dining rooms, breakfast room, four good bedrooms, two attics, bath-room, outbuildings, stables, coach house, saddle room, &c., found a purchaser for £650 in Mr. Thomas Houldsworth. Lot 5, eight dwelling-houses and outbuildings, and 1a. 2r. 6p. of grass land, in Clay Lane, and producing a rental of £58 8s. per year, was withdrawn at £480. The remaining lots, ten building plots of 1,240 yards, 1,074, 677, 383, 448, 480, 377, 620, 408, and 666 square yards respectively, did not tempt a bid. Lot 1 and several other lots have since been disposed of. Mr. John Bunting, Chesterfield, was the solicitor in the matter.

Park Villa was described as a newly erected residence in May 1880 when it was auctioned off and purchased by Thomas Holdsworth for £650. This house was built for George Froggatt who resided at the Poplars on Bestwood. In 1881, George Goodwin, mineral agent, lived there, followed by William Drabble in 1890, Anne Thorpe in 1911 and then Thomas Collings, cab proprietor. In April 1972 George and Joe Holmes' Coaches Ltd established their business here.

Purchase of Park Villa, June 1888.

Some of the Drabble family outside Park Villa, c. 1900. This post card was sent to Master H. Drabble at Park Villa. The 1891 census records an Eleanor Drabble, born in Manchester, with children William, Harry, Annie, Dorothy, Catherine, Lucy and two servants Bertha Collings and Matilda Coup. All the children were born at Pilsley and they appear to have moved into Park Villa in 1888.

A view looking up Market Street, c. 1900. This street was named after the Co-op markets and hall built in 1868, but the streets were not officially named by the Local Board of Health until October 1876. The Co-op also established a pig market in Market Street in about 1874. In July 1929, the Old Kino Hall covered-in market was opened up again, but without much success, and in 1932 the open market was restablished in Market Street. The present open market commenced in 1980.

Market Street, 1974. Baskill's received planning permission to convert three shops (Nos 13-15) into their television centre in September 1964. Baskill's closed in 1989, having sold out to Bennett and Fountain, a Kent based electrical company. Marshall's were receiving television pictures in 1935 from Alexandra Palace but did not sell their first commercial television until 1949, to Joe Brown, a Holmgate farmer.

The Furnace Inn, 1986, prior to its renovation with Raymond Whittaker as landlord. Its name derives from the CXC furnaces and it was built around 1850. Charles Roper was the landlord in 1870 and, according to the 1871 census, George Leivers, keeper of the furnace, was lodging there. The pubs's name was changed to the Old English in November 1987.

An advert from the *Derbyshire Times*, December 1862, referring to London House in Wingfield Road.

A reference to Mantle Lane and a 'valuable bed of Ironstone and seams of Coal' for sale in December 1841. These two roads are referred to on the tithe plan as Cox's Top Close and Cox's Bottom, and relate to Thomas Cock the owner.

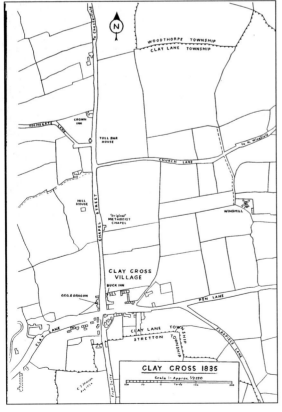

Froggatts Row, Market Street, c. 1976. The stone part of this row is shown on the 1841 town plan with the brick houses being added later. This row was demolished in 1981 to make way for the council bungalows but the stone wall feature has been retained. The Froggatts were large property owners in the town and their family vault is at North Wingfield. In 1881 Thomas Holland kept a beerhouse in this particular row.

A plan of Clay Lane Township in 1835, showing Church Lane with no development when it was probably just used as a burial route to North Wingfield church and for access to Hay's windmill.

Three
Eyre Street

yre Street 1976. This street was named after Eire because a good many Southern Irish people
ved here during the 1860s. In January 1868 the Fenian Brotherhood was active in the area and
guard was put on the Clay Cross tunnel. About thirty police raided 'Irish Street' late in the
ight and a strict search of nearly every house was made for arms and combustibles. Several
embers of the Clay Cross Volunteers were sworn in as special constables. Most of these houses
ere back-to-back houses which were notoriously unhygienic: in July 1914, all the owners of
ich houses were given twelve months to install some through ventilation or be issued with a
osing order. In September 1955, fourteen houses in this street were declared unfit for human
abitation and were promptly demolished. In 1959 the surveyor was instructed to lay out plans
r a car park on 875 sq yds of land purchased for £325.

This street was also referred to as 'Black Horse Street' after the pub that was once situated in th town's Working Mens' Club. In February 1911 the club was struck off the register for eightee months by the Alfreton magistrates for a breach of licensing laws. In 1921 planning permissio was given to improve and alter the premises. Once again, in January 1934, the club was struc off the register for twelve months for selling retail beer without a license.

Some of the last houses being demolished in Eyre Street in 1964 to make way for the Blue Dyk surgery, built the following year. In 1861 this particular street had five lodging houses. In 189 the first house, coming down the street on the left, was occupied by Samuel Stoppard, his wi Elizabeth and their six children. Several two roomed houses are also recorded in 'Black Hor Yard'.

A view from Market Street overlooking Eyre Street, showing Bridge Street and Office Row, with the Concrete Houses to the right in front of the Ready Mix plant. The back-to-back Concrete Houses are not named after the Ready Mix Plant but are recorded as such in the 1881 census. Bridge Street was partly built from stone that was salvaged from the demolition of the Coneygreen Bridge when the Erewash Line was built in 1860 – hence Bridge Street.

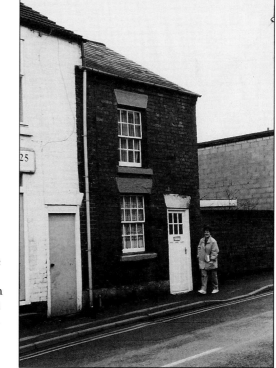

One of the remaining cottages in Eyre Street, retaining its original windows, which was built by a speculator builder during the boom of the mid-1850s. Before the advent of any local government in the town, the sanitary conditions were appalling with open sewers and cesspits. In September 1868, a young Irish child, John Garraty, had a narrow escape when he fell into a ten feet deep open cesspit that was full to the depth of four feet; this cesspit was situated in Eyre Street.

SALE OF INNKEEPER'S FIXTURES, FITT-
INGS, UTENSILS and EFFECTS.
"BLACK HORSE" INN, EYRE ST., CLAY
CROSS.

MESSRS. WM. WATSON & SON have received instructions from Mr. T. Britton
(who is leaving the premises, the License having
been taken by Statutory Powers) to SELL upon
the above premises, on

TUESDAY, DECEMBER 24th, 1907.

Whole of the MAHOGANY-FRAMED SEAT-
ING in Parlour, in A.C. with Head-rail, Arm-
rests, etc. 31ft., 16 Boston Stools, Box Forms, 2
Oblong Tables, various Pictures, Gas Brackets
with incandescent fittings, Bagatelle Board,
Skittle Board, 2-handled Pint Cans, 1-handled
½-pint Can, Pewter Measures, Painted Double
Cupboard, Secretaire with 4 Cash Drawers,
Deal-top Counter with inside shelving, cash
drawer and key; Bar Fixture with glassed win-
dows, doors, etc., Counter with mahogany top,
3 Mahogany-framed Bar Tables with inlaid tops
on metal standards, Smoke Chair, Painted
Corner Cupboard, Settle with 2 arm rests, Ob-
long Table, Set Brass-rail Iron Bedsteads, 6
Hair-seated Chairs, Set Iron Bedsteads, Pair
Straw Mattresses, Wool Bed, Painted Wash-
stand, large double-fronted Cupboard, Metal
Fenders, Upholstered Mahogany Seat 4ft.,
Window Rollers and Blinds, Mahogany Cigar
Box, 3 Crib Boards, Venetian Ashes Pans, Steel-
rim Fender, Lino on floors, Mahogany Wind
Screen, Wine Kegs, Fireirons, Couch in A.C.,
Table with O.C. cover, Set Steps, Table Tops,
Trestles, 3 Round Tables, Seating in A.C.,
Wood Shelving, Lamp and Fittings, Metal Pan
and underworks, Timber forming Pig Stye, Sign
and lettering, and other effects.

Sale to commence at 1 p.m.

Auction and Valuation Offices:
Alfreton, Ripley and Clay Cross

Sale of innkeeper's fixtures and fittings, Black
Horse Inn, December 1907.

Harriet and John Downing's shop,
Eyre Street, c. 1976, with 'YZ' 1d
gift machines on the gable end.
They aquired this particular shop
in about 1933 and purchased it off
Stoppards – whether or not this is
the same Stoppards mentioned in
the 1891 census returns is not yet
known. The landlord of the Black
Horse Inn at this date was George
Whileman.

Four
Thanet Street

Thanet Street from the High Street Junction showing Mrs Marsh, a member of the New Connection Methodist church, leading the 1962 Whitsuntide procession. Winnie Kimes's shop can be seen close to the traffic lights with the Brooke Bond Tea sign above the door. The five houses in this row were built in 1855 and were the property of Thomas Wilson. At this date they were occupied by Messers J. Roberts, J. Rooth, W. Wild, C. Hunt and Mr Burns. The sale for this property on 11 February 1856, was held at the George and Dragon and 'The above property is situate at the Cross Roads at Old Clay Cross, suitable for business of any description in so flourshing a town.'

A journey continuing up Thanet Street commences with a shop that was once called the 'Dusty Miller' pub, which was built about 1856. In more recent times it was Thurnham's betting shop. The journey continues with Elsie Reddishes', Joe Garraty's and Longmate's butchers shop. In 1871 George Elliott was landlord of the Dusty Miller and by 1891, it was Jediah Wood.

Mr W.A. Webster, landlord of the Dusty Miller pub in 1910, which at this time was owned by G. Elliott and leased to the Chesterfield Brewery. The license for this pub was taken away under the Confiscation Act in July 1910. It was the last of the pre-1869 beerhouses to be dealt with by the Derbyshire Compensation Authority and was awarded £1,368. The average annual sale over a period of five years was 186 barrels and 138 dozen bottles.

A group of Dusty Miller regulars enjoying the last drinks before the pub lost its license. The Elliotts, who owned this pub, were millers who also ran the water and then the steam corn mill in Mill Lane – hence the name Dusty Miller. 'The ale traffic in Clay Cross is doing more injury to the miner than his working eleven to twelve hours per day – only think there are 23 public houses in the midst of Clay Cross, besides the outskirts where the men often go on a Sunday, when they ought to be at some place of worship'.

A 'blitzkrieg' of another part of Thanet Street almost opposite the Prince of Wales and showing a glimpse into Elliotts Yard. The demolition contract for Nos 33 - 45 Thanet Street (seven houses), Nos 13 - 23a Thanet Street (eight houses) and Nos 49 - 61 Elliotts Yard, was awarded to A. Buckland on 23 February 1970, at £20 per dwelling. A total of thirty-eight other properties on Grundy Road and King Street were demolished by L.J. Harris for £684.

A view of the same area looking from the opposite side of the road and depicting the Prince o Wales with the new Pankhurst Place development in the background, that would rehouse some of the Thanet Street and King Street tenants. Authorisation for plans to be prepared for the Pankhurst project was given on 11 November 1963; forty-five flats and maisonettes were completed in September 1969.

Thanet House, the home of Dr John Barnard Lee, who came to Clay Cross from Crich in 1869 Dr Lee married Annie Howe, only daughter of William Howe (snr), CXC engineer and the had four children. Dr Lee died on 21 January 1919, at Thanet House. This house was purchased by J. Spriggs, printer, for £880 in March 1924, and is now incorporated into the Catholic Church building and used as a so-called Job Club.

Dr John Barnard Lee (seated with umberella), with some of his family. The young boy standing is Alfred Slack who started the solicitor's practice in Clay Cross and Chesterfield. Dr Lee was medical officer for the Pilsley Company's Field Club and public vaccinator to the Chesterfield Union. He was born at Crich in 1842 and died 21 January 1919, and buried in Clay Cross Cemetery.

In September 1967, it was resolved 'that King Street, Grundy Road development phases 1, 2 and 3 be named Pankhurst Place', after Emily Pankhurst the suffragette. The ministry's architect insisted that solid fuel fires should not be used in this development. In May 1966, phase one of fifteen units was awarded to A. Pearson for £33,880; the other two phases were also awarded to Pearson for £33,680 and £42,580 respectively.

Thanet Street, Clay Cross

Thanet Street was named after the Earl of Thanet, one of the Lords of Stretton Manor. Prior to this the road was called Wingfield Mill Lane and Pen Lane. A water-powered corn mill can be traced back to 1086 on the site at the bottom of Hagg Hill at Parkhouse. The landlord of the Queens Head named on this postcard is S.A. Thorpe and before this, in 1904, it was George Thorpe. In August 1862, Mr William Dore aquired a new licence at the Alfreton Brewster Sessions and, in 1871, he was recorded as an innkeeper and farmer of seventeen acres. William Handley was landlord in 1892, with Henry Lander in 1900, James Cresswell in 1908, Harry Fuller in 1912 and Thomas Kinder in 1922.

Cross Street, built around the mid-1850s and looking on to King Street (New Street) from Thanet Street, features some of the earliest speculators' buildings in the town. Between April 1962 and June 1963, several Cross Street properties were aquired by the UDC and the demolition contract was awarded to Roger Ryan. Miss E. Chambers was the owner of some of the Cross Street properties which she sold to the UDC for £200, plus payment of £14 14s surveyor's fees. James Haslam, the town's first MP and DMA secretary, once lived in this street.

Looking down King Street (New Street), c. 1950 with the corner of Cross Street to the right. The 1891 census records that at the end of Cross Street and beginning of New Street, the first three houses were used as a lodging house with John Phillips as the head of 'household'; together with his wife and two servants there were twenty-four lodgers – 'please wipe your feet when you go out'.

Another view of King Street taken from the High Street junction during preparations for the 1953 Coronation, with Sylvia and Fred Barlow's motor-bike shop on the right. Part of the tall building on the right was once the Salvation Army Hall and is recorded as such in March 1912. Barlow's shop was originally Slack's butchers, then Joseph Lester's. During the Second World War some army officers were billeted there, then it became Morton's Motorbike shop before the Barlows took it over.

Shakey Yard was named after the Shakespeare Inn built, c. 1850. This particular area was known as Monkey Park in the 1851 and 1861 census returns and the bottom block of houses, behind the family group, was called Milton Street. The Shakespeare Inn gave up its license with the Confiscation Act of 1903 and was converted into a lodging house in 1908 – also known as Shaw's Yard. Isaac Shaw was a lodging house keeper in Monkey Park in 1871 with twenty-two lodgers resident.

This book is the second of a possible three volumes that will contribute to the town's visual archive and is indebted to Albert Heath, the photographer who took many of the early images. A native of Clay Cross, he first worked at the Parkhouse Colliery and then set up as a professional photographer in Thanet Street in 1904. He served with the local Volunteers and Territorials for about twelve years, with twenty months active service in France and Eygpt with the Cyclist Corps. He died in August 1917, aged 37.

Main Street at Danesmoor, c. 1920, derives its name from Ainmoor which was the name of the Stretton manorial commons. The earliest reference to 'Dainsmoor commonly called Anemoor' appears in William Cowlishaw's will of 1768. The North Wingfield parish registers show that from about 1780, these two place names were used synonymously with the same families for recording their rights of passage. Old Danesmoor was situated on the Gents Hill area.

Barbara, Sue and Val in 1964 at Danesmoor with the 'Catty' tip in the background. The plans for the Ingham's factory were submitted for planning permission in January 1962 and building was completed in 1963. A compulsory purchase was made on the Primitive Methodist Chapel in February 1966, which was demolished sometime in 1967. The Parkhouse Hotel, Bottom Pub, was built around 1872 by Mr Hodgkinson, a local businessman.

The Square at Danesmoor built by George Hoffman, pork butcher, who came to Clay Cross from Germany in about 1860 and who, together with his wife Catherine, was 'naturalised' by 1871. The census at this date records him as a pork butcher and farmer of sixty acres employing two men. They had four children: Ludwig, George, Louise and John. Catherine died in 1932 at Poulton Street, Kirkham, Lancashire, at the age of 89 years.

In June 1962, several houses in the Square (Nos 20 to 30) were condemned to be demolished by a UDC Clearance Order and in March 1968, Nos 51 to 61, and Nos 1, 2 and 5 were also ordered to be demolished. For some considerable time the Hoffmans were absentee landlords and there are numerous references in the Clay Cross UDC minutes ordering them to improve their property or be faced with a closing order.

Pawnshop tickets – to the Manor born!.

Five

Shops and Small Businesses

Frank Kenning, founder of the Kenning's empire, Clay Cross, in 1878. He was a self made man and was a native of Clay Cross, born on 15 February 1854 and died on 7 December 1905. He started work in the pit at an early age and when the rope 'kinged' he decided to leave the pit and began business as a hawker. He married Ann Whitworth in 1872 and they had seven children: Eliza-Ann, Mary-Elizabeth, Frank, George, Lavinia, Lillie and Herbert. Frank Kenning (snr) was the first Chairman of the Clay Cross UDC (1894 to 1905) and this particular portrait was hung in the UDC office by his son George in recognition of his father's service and benevolence to the town and its people.

Frank Kenning (jnr) with a young helper, *c.* 1900, doing their rounds. In May 1868, George Kenning, pot hawker of Clay Cross, was charged by PC Newton with allowing his horse to stray onto the highway at Newmarket. ' The defendant admitted the charge, and expressed the hope that the magistrates would deal leniently with him, as he had been fined thirty-nine times, and so had been a good customer to them'. He was fined 5s and 11s 6d costs and said, ' he would pay the money as soon as he had sold some pots he had in the market, but a distress warrant was issued'.

An auction notice by W.R. Nutt in August 1910, regarding the sale of their horses 'owing to having purchased motor lorry and car'.

George Kenning's very first car was aquired by collecting several thousand Queen's Honey soap wrappers and then trading them in for a car. As part of their business they sold and promoted this soap product and persuaded customers to sell them the wrappers at 2½d per dozen.

Frank Kenning's confectionary shop in New Street (King Street), *c*. 1880s. Several of the Kenning family came to Clay Cross during the late 1830s from Melbourne, near Derby. Abraham Kenning was recorded as a putter in 1841 and by 1851 he was a licensed hawker. In 1861 George Kenning, Frank's grandfather, was recorded as an earthenware dealer and so was his uncle Jacob.

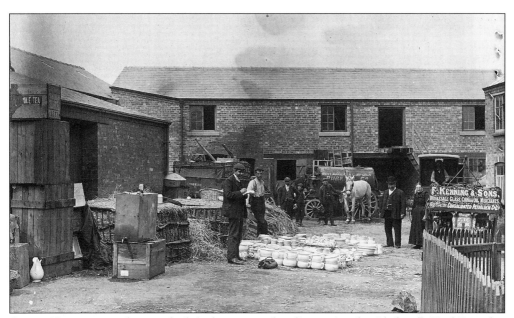

George Kenning, standing on the left, doing an audit of 'jerries' in the Gladstone Yard Complex which incorporated Gladstone House, built, c. 1897. It was to the oil business that George owed his first steps in the business world. The earliest agreement for the distribution of oil products was made in 1903 with the Anglo Caucasian Oil Company and later amalgamated to become Shell Max and BP Ltd. Their petroleum licence was approved in August 1881.

Another view into the hardware depot on Revill Street, now Broadleys, c. 1900. In March 1908, George Kenning, who succeeded his father has head of the business, decided to purchase two neighbouring properties in New Street but by this date their main business had moved to the Gladstone Buildings and to the Albert Buildings on High Street.

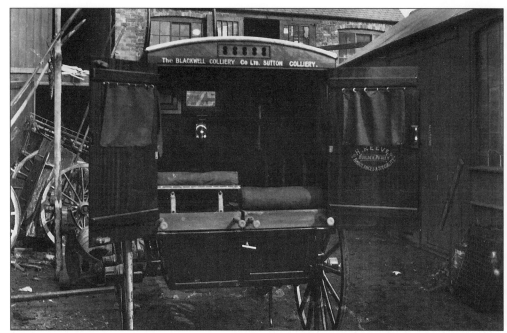

In 1925, George Kenning was taken into partnership with the Reeve Company at Pilsley and the company name was altered to Messrs Reeve and Kenning. The foundation of this particular firm was established in 1888 by Harry Reeve, coach builder and wheelwright, whose name became a household word amongst the users of horse vehicles of every kind. However, it was the motor vehicle trade led by George Kenning that expanded and secured the business.

A Morris Commercial 1930, sold at the Clay Cross depot – 'The Middleweight Champion of the World has knocked out all competition.' This particular truck could be purchased for £249 10s or by the 'MC' hire purchase plan of a £45 down payment which included tax and insurance for one year. This 30 cwt truck, when loaded to capacity, could climb a gradient of 1 in $2\frac{1}{2}$, would reach a speed of 45 mph and would economise on running to the extent of 16 to 19 mpg, so the advert claimed.

KENNINGS, LTD., TO BE PUBLIC COMPANY

Motor Firm With Depots in Six Counties

After 60 years' trading as a family concern the famous firm of Kennings, Ltd., is to become a public limited company.

Towards the end of this month and the reason, it is stated, is to make the concern, which already has 19 depots in six counties.

an issue is to be made to the public, provision for future developments of

The "Sheffield Telegraph" understands that the nominal capital of the company will be £500,000 of which £200,000 will be 5½ per cent. Cumulative £1 Preference shares and £300,000 will be issued in 1,200,000 Ordinary 5s. shares.

Of the Preference shares £100,000 will be issued to the public at part and of the Ordinary shares 350,000 will be issued to the public at 7s. 6d.

The capital cover of the Preference shares is 3½ times, and the dividend cover nearly 8½ times on the basis of the average for the last four years and 12½ times on the basis of last year's profits.

After providing for Preference dividends the balance of profit represents more than 19 per cent. on the whole of the issued share capital or nearly 13 per cent. on the price of the Ordinary shares.

MANAGERS TAKING SHARES

Special provision is being made for 100,000 ordinary shares to be reserved for managers of Kennings, Ltd.

The issue is being made to mark the diamond jubilee of the firm, which was founded by the late Mr. Frank Kenning, who was in the glass and china trade.

Mr. Frank Kenning, senior, died in 1905, the business being taken over by his sons, Mr. Frank Kenning and Mr. George Kenning. In 1908, when Mr. Frank Kenning junior died, Mr. George Kenning was joined by his younger brother who still carries on the hardware business.

In 1910 Mr. George Kenning entered

[Photo: Ethel M. Eadon.

MR. GEORGE KENNING

Saturday 14 May 1938, *Derby Telegraph.*

53

A share cheque for the Clay Cross Co-operative that was established in New Street around 1859, under the title of the Clay Cross Pioneer Industrial Society and which continued to flourish throughout the nineteenth century until it was eventually taken over by the Chesterfield Co-op in July 1930.

A view of the Clay Cross Co-op from Market Street junction, c. 1937. The society purchased part of these premises on High Street in 1860 and 1863. The first few years were difficult and the members considered giving up, but they pressed on and in 1868, the society was reported to be in a very prosperous condition with 150 members and a paid up capital of £1,716. In 1863 they paid their first dividend and registered with the 'Act'. In 1874 they celebrated the opening of their first drapery store.

The Co-op Market Hall opened in July 1869 – 'for the benefit of the townspeople and tradesmen'. This building was 170 ft long, 40 ft wide and incorporated some 1,300 square feet of glass at a cost of £400. George Howe, CXC engineer, was the architect and the iron roof supports were made by the CXC under the supervision of Mr Wilkinson. The other contractors were Mr Mycroft (woodwork), Mr Udall, (plumbing and glazing), Mr Hays (brickwork) and Mr Cutts (masonery work).

The Eyre Street end of the Market Hall (Old Kino Hall) during demolition work in 1987/88. Prior to its demolition it housed Spriggs, the old Clay Cross printing firm, was a motorbike workshop for Eric Housley and at one time was a small hosiery factory for Stocktons.

Bell's Stores, 1908, situated at 2 High Street, opposite the Elm Tree Inn. Unfortunately very little information has been found about this shop other than a couple of adverts – see opposite.

An advert for Bell's Stores from the *Clay Cross Chronicle*, March 1908.

Another view of Bell's shop from the Market Street junction. According to the 1891 census returns the shops in this view were those of Robert Oxley (stationer), John Smith (chemist), Catherine Nutt (general dealer), George Bescoby (grocer), Charles Atkinson (draper), Job Brough (beerhouse keeper of the Red Lion), William Marshall (pork butcher), John Nixon (grocery manager at the Star Tea Company) and William Sears (keeper of the Star Hotel).

The Albert Buildings situated on the High Street were built in about 1852 and named after Prince Albert. This view shows William Slack's butchers shop, Richard Marshall's cycle shop, Kenning's confectionery and tea shop and Senior's pawn shop at the end of the row preparing for a redemption sale – 'Great sale of unredeemed pledges every Monday at 2.30 am and every Thursday at 5.30 am.' Marshall's cycle shop was once used as lock-up for the Derbyshire Constabulary and in 1871, Dennis Gorman (police inspector) resided there.

William Slack posing with his family outside their shop, *c.* 1890 at the New Street junction. William established his business at Clay Cross in 1853 and Kelly's Directory, 1895, records him as a family butcher, purveyor of cattle, cattle dealer and farmer. He was a breeder of greyhounds and took an avid interest in coursing; he was elected to the first Local Board of Health in 1875 and sat for some twenty years. At the Alfreton Petty Sessions in April 1863, William Slack and William Mycroft were appointed the last parish constables for the township of Clay Lane.

Haslam's shoe shop in Market Street. William Haslam (snr) was born in 1814 and came to Clay Cross in 1841, where he established a shoe making business in Market Street and employed about fifty hand sewing bootmakers. The business had a tannery at Brackenfield and a currier shop at Higham which had been in the Haslam family for about 200 years. They continued to make boots by hand until 1870, when machinery was introduced. The premises shown here were opened in 1865.

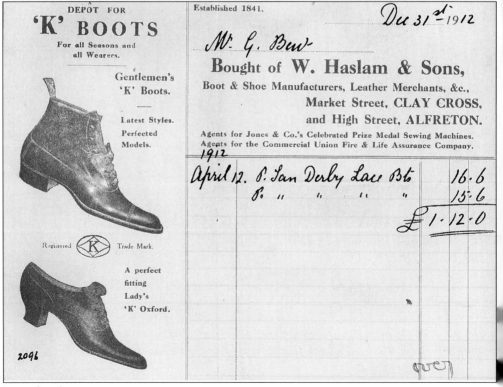

Letter head.

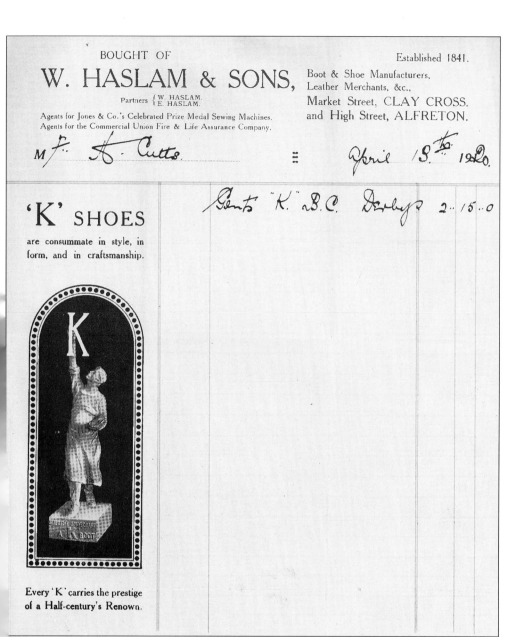

M/ F. H. Cutts.   =   April 15th 1920.

Gents 'K' B.C. Derbys   2..15..0

Another bill head for 31 December 1912.

William Lomas, general ironmonger, established his business in Market Street in 1875 afte working in the local colleries. William was a dedicated New Connection Methodist and died ir February 1910, to be succeeded by his son George Lomas. The business was incorporated as a Limited Company in 1954, but was wound up as such when Frank Lomas retired from the hardware department in 1988. The card shop aspect of the business was established in 1980 and Tony Lomas retired from this in May 1996.

A later photograph showing George standing outside the shop with two adverts in the window for 'Hardy's Picks and Boring Machines', 'Skelton's Spades, Shovels and Garden Tools' and 'Tyzac's and Turner's Celebrated Hand Saws'. Also at this date glass and china had been introduced in competition with Frank Kenning. These shop fronts were substantially altered in 1923 and soon after a warehouse was added which was later to became the Toy Shop selling Triang toys.

An advert in the *Clay Cross Chronicle* for July 1900.

note in the *Derbyshire Courier* for March 1862.

A portrait of Arthur Henry Cornford (1862-1903) – 'The People's Draper' – whose shop was next to the George and Dragon. (see page 22) After seeing the business up for sale in *The Drapers Record* he purchased the business and came up from Torquay to Clay Cross in 1890. According to the 1891 census returns his wife had not joined him at this date. He was born in Maidstone, Kent.

Mary Cornford *née* Southwell was born in Lincoln in 1868. She and her husband had six children: Fredrick, Violet, Ivy, Myrtle, Daisy and Henry. After her husband's death in November 1903, she sold the business and moved into a cottage in Lower Market Street and subsequently aquired the Egstow Post Office which she managed for thirty-two years. The first post office at Egstow was opened up in 1904 in Egstow Street and managed by Mr W. Banks.

Arthur and Mary Cornford with their eldest son Fredrick, in the landau which Arthur used to commute to his other shop in Bulwell, Nottinghamshire. He was a friend of Frank Kenning who frequently accompanied him to the Chesterfield races. Arthur also frequented the George and Dragon pub next door and would hire a room there at Christmas to entertain family and friends.

MARKET STREET,
CLAY CROSS, *April 30*

M{ru} Banks

THOMAS COLLINGS,
Cab, Carriage & Waggonette Proprietor.

All Branches of Posting undertaken,   School Treats, Pic-nic Parties, etc., catered for.   Cabs to Station
at any hour, at short notice.   ✿   ✿   ✿   Charges Strictly Moderate.

£

Shellibeer & 3 Coaches in Attendence
to M{ru} Banks Funeral   *£ 1*

Received the Above

Thomas Collings

With thanks

Thomas Collings' bill head, 30 April 1906.

TELEPHONE: CHESTERFIELD 2767 & 76441

ESTABLISHED 1871

W. D. BOTHAM & SONS

WM. C. BOTHAM, F.A.I.   W. D. BOTHAM, F.A.I.
J. K. BOTHAM   J. E. SHEMWELL F.A.I.

AUCTIONEERS, ESTATE AGENTS, VALUERS & SURVEYORS

71, LOW PAVEMENT, CHESTERFIELD.

Instructed by Mr. G. Collings.   PARTICULARS OF PROPERTY FOR SALE BY AUCTION

PARK VILLA, 124 MARKET STREET

CLAY CROSS, CHESTERFIELD

W. D. BOTHAM & SONS WILL SELL BY AUCTION

THE HORSE DRAWN VEHICLES, HARNESS,

LAMPS, WHEELS AND SURPLUS HOUSEHOLD

FURNITURE AND EFFECTS

on

WEDNESDAY, 11th NOVEMBER, 1970

at

1 p.m. prompt.

A fine old horse drawn Hearse complete with steels and velvet drapes for either single or double horse. A very good heavy two wheel show cart, Old Hearse body.   2 Harvest drays on spoke wheels. 2 carts on pneumatics, trailer carts on solid wheels, hand cart, 2 heavy carts, Cart body, various shafts.

P.T.O.

All negotiations to be made through W. D. Botham and Sons.

MISREPRESENTATIONS ACT 1967

Particulars of property for sale by auction for Mr G. Collings, 11 November 1970.

Thomas Collings bringing in passengers to the Picture Palace at Clay Cross to view 'The world famous Dixie Kid, Olive Melba, Jemmons Marionettes, Marionette Matinee and Lillie Soutter. Time and Prices as usual'. Thomas, a native of Cinderhill, Nottinghamshire, came to Clay Cross with his parents when he was 3 years old. He was taught by James Stollard until aged 8 and then worked at the CXC No. 2 Pit until he was 23 years of age. He then commenced work as a grocer and general smallware dealer in Froggatts Row, Market Street. At the age of 43 he launched out as a bus and cab proprietor and moved to Park Villa, Market Street and retired in 1919. Together with his father Joseph and his wife Isabella, an accomplished violinist, they contributed regularly to chapel anniversaries. They were married at Clay Cross Parish Church on 3 December 1880, and celebrated their Golden Wedding in 1930 at Bonsall where they had retired. George and Joe Holmes Coaches Ltd established their business at Park Villa in April 1972.

Simon Holmes (snr), in his wheelchair outside his shop in New Street. Simon came to Clay Cross around 1863 from Ibstock in Leicestershire. He was seriously injured in 1868 at Messrs Smith and Shepherds' colliery at Danesmoor when the cage plummeted to the bottom. The local Friendly Society had a collection for him when his 'club money' ran out which he invested in setting up this small shop in New Street.

White's shop on the Broadleys and Thanet Street Junction in 1963. Joseph Henry White established his grocery and provision store here in 1890 and after his demise in October 1935, his son-in-law Edward Clay managed the business. At one time Mr White was chairman of the UDC, a governor of Clay Cross Secondary School and a member of the Board of the Isolation Hospital.

Henry Marshall posing with The Lily outside their Clay Cross Cycle and Motor Works situated in Eldon Street with the showroom on High Street, built, c. 1900. The bike was named after his mother Lily and was built about 1912. Richard Marshall established his business as a watchmaker and jeweller in Clay Cross in 1870 and at this date he constructed his first iron velocipede. In November 1902, a report in the *Clay Cross Chronicle* reads 'On visiting the workrooms of Messrs R. Marshall and Sons this week we were pleased to note that we had a cycle manufacturer who was up to date. We found in the shop a dynamo, every part which had been made by Mr Marshall and Sons, including the fitting and the armature and the winding of the field magnetic coil.' Henry was born in 1842 at Heage and came to Clay Cross in 1869, where he first began work in one of the local pits.

Mrs Emma Marshall, Henry's sister, holding a Minerva powered motor cycle, *c.* 1906. She was reputed to be the first lady motor cyclist in Derbyshire.

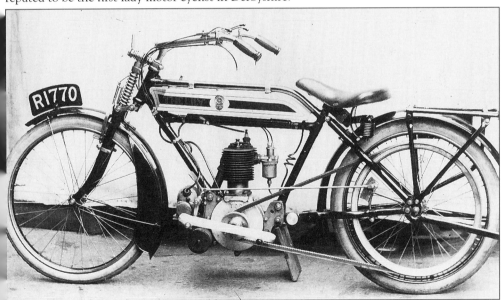

The Lily with a $3\frac{1}{2}$ hp T.D. Cross engine, B & B carburettor, Bosch magneto and built on what appears to be a Campion frame of 1912-13. The badge on the petrol tank reads 'R. Marshall & Sons, Maker, High Street, Clay Cross' but the bikes were really purchased either in kit form or made up from various parts purchased from small-time motor cycle makers. This business was only a side line and not more than twenty appear to have been made.

Mrs Renshaw outside her grocery and fruiterers shop in Dores Yard, later called Peters Square. Note the remains of an Ashover Light Railway poster below the shop sign. John Renshaw started this shop after being blacklisted by the CXC for his trade union activity. After a strike at the Parkhouse Pit which lasted fourteen weeks in support of John Renshaw – 'the only pit that has ever stood for one man' – he convinced the men to return to work and they collected enough money to set him up with a horse and cart.

Mr Thomas Greaves, son of Benjamin Greaves of Stourton Grange, Hunslet, came to Clay Cross in 1881 to manage Senior's pawnbroking establishment. In 1898 he set up his own business and opened a shop in Market Street selling house furniture. In 1932 his firm began to manufacture upholstered furniture employing about six men, which soon increased to twenty-two and, in November 1936, he opened a new upholstery factory on Bridge Street.

An advert in the *Clay Cross Chronicle*, 10 July 1910.

William Smith, cash grocer, outside his shop at the corner of Stollard Street and Market Street. He emigrated to Canada in May 1906 and settled in the district of Forestburg and Heisler. Stollard Street was named after Joseph Stollard, the CXC company school teacher (1862-1892), who aquired much property in this area. He died in September 1906 and is buried in the Wingerworth churchyard.

A family photograph of the Smith family prior to their emigration to Canada. William Smith was choirmaster at the Clay Cross Wesleyan Chapel who presented him with a purse of gold at a farewell gathering. Tom Smith, grocer, one of his sons (standing centre) also emigrated to the same district of Canada in 1929 and present at the reunion there were, including grandchildren and great-grandchildren, forty-eight members of the family.

James W. Petts, printer, situated on the north-east side of High Street and now the Indian 'takeaway'. Little is known about master printer James Petts other than he was born in Halifax and came to Clay Cross from Killarmarsh. He does not appear in Kelly's 1912 Directory but printed John Renshaw's election phamplet in 1919. The poster in the window is for a 'Grand Dance' with the Kit Kat Band, held at North Wingfield Church School Rooms.

Thomas William Thorpe, fruit and potato dealer, Eyre Street, standing with his first wife Maria. Thomas' father George was a native of Denby Common, Derby and lived in Clay Cross for twenty-five years. He worked as a miner for eighteen years and was landlord of the Queens Head pub for seven years. George died from gangrene, 17 May 1909, at the age of 58, in the Nottingham General Hospital. Thomas was landlord of the Shoulder of Mutton, Clay Cross, on two occasions and had a life-long interest in horse dealing.

William Thorpe's shop, No. 124 High Street, situated below Pleasant Row and opposite Cellar Row. This shop was owned by Bradley, the local timber merchant, and Thomas moved into this shop sometime in 1936. The person walking down the High Street is Bud Guilding, the local grave digger. He once told some of the Elm Tree tap-room customers that he had sailed on the biggest ship in the world – 'Hardship'.

Tommy Thorpe (jnr) and Vincent Hodgkinson renovating one of their carts at the back of their shop on High Street, showing the infants school to the left and the gable end of Shakey Yard Row, the front doors of which faced onto the schoolyard. The Thorpes frequently offered their services at Whitsuntide to convey the Gospel Mission, Sunday School or Salvation scholars around the town.

A cheerful Sam Thorpe outside the family shop on High Street, loaded up ready to do his rounds assisted by his brother Tommy. Besides 'hawking' his fruit and vegetables, Sam also worked as a collier at the Holmewood and Arkwright collieries. He is an enthusiastic member of the Chesterfield Male Voice Choir, Clay Cross Fellowship Choir and Chesterfield Operatic Society. After many years in the hawking trade that started with his father, they finally stopped trading around 1985.

Aug 3 1911

Mr W. Haslam

Bought of A. MAYCOCK
TAILOR &c.
Gents.' Clothing cleaned and neatly repaired.

June 12 repairing & Cleaning Hat & Tro	2/6
June 14 repairing Nickers	4
June 16 repairing Suit	1 6
July 10 repairing Suit	2/.
July 23 Cleaning & Repairing Suit	2/6
July 31st repairing Top Coat & Tro	6
Aug 3 new pipe in Tro	6
	9/10
Cash Paid	1. 0
	8. 10

Paid W. Nickers
Aug 3 / 11

(8/10 to Cr. of a/c)

Six
Community

King Street, 1937. It was in 1911 that New Street was renamed King Street when it won the best decorated street competition for the George V Coronation. The *Derbyshire Times* reported that 'Mr Kenning is providing souvenir mugs for the children while the beacon, which will have an accompaniment of rockets, is being provided by Brigadier General G.M. Jackson. A prize is offered to the best dressed street and residents and trades people are being asked to decorate their premises as they did on the occasion of the Jubilee'. The town's community bonfires were usually held on the No. 1 Pit tip situated behind behind the Kwik Save store and Waterloo Street.

King Street decorated on 12 May 1937, for the coronation of George VI when it again won the best decorated street competition. The CXC gave out money to about 5,000 of their empoyees with adults receiving 8s, youths between 18 and 20 years, 5s and those under 18 years, 3s each. Workers temporarily indisposed owing to accident or illness received similar amounts and those incapacitated for over six months were given 3s.

King Street preparing for the 1953 Coronation competition which they also won for being the best decorated street in the district. An iron plaque made by the CXC was erected in King Street on 29 November and was unveiled by Peggy and Joan Jackson. Mr H. Smith of No. 87 High Street, also agreed to the fixing of a Coronation Clock above his shop. The clock is now situated on the Victoria Buildings, depleted of the crown but with a pit headstocks in its place.

Brampton Brewery off licence, 26 King Street. The proprietors at this date were Fred and Minnie Hooper. At the left of the picture are Mrs Armstrong, George Albert Hooper, George Hooper, Barry Hooper and Ivy Smith.

The Salvation Army Coronation dray 1953, outside the New Inn, Market Street, being pulled by Tommy Thorpe's horse. The tall lad on the far left is Cyril Milner. From left to right on the dray: Margaret Stephens, Margaret Mogford, Christine Bramley, Madeline White, Pat Worthy, Terry Hooper (front), Dennis Whitmore, Tommy Collier, Trevor Bradshaw. Seated: Mrs Liza Simpson. Behind the chair on the left: John Raywood. To the right of Mrs Simpson: John Greenfield, Violet Greenfield and May Greenfield.

Salvation Army dray on the 1963, Whit Walk. Front left: Doris Mogford. Back row from left to right: Timothy Fellows, Marie Churm, Angela Poole, Veronica Dickens, Barbara Poole, -?-, Joanne McCreedy, Sheena Kerry, Christine Kirman. Front row from left to right: Beverly Hooper, Gale Bradbury, Jill Walker, ? Broomhall, Gale Bramley and Janet Porter.

Mr William Quemby posing as Old King Cole in the carnival of August 1932. The block of coal was brought from 1½ miles underground from the No. 2 Pit and this was organised by the under manager, Mr Sharman. A competition was held to guess the weight of the coal and was won by Mr J. Shaw of No. 52 Market Street, who guessed the exact weight of 26 cwt 56 lb and 7 oz. On this occasion Miss Hilda Watson was the Carnival Queen and George Eyre the Carnival King.

Clay Cross Carnival procession, August 1935, which was an event organised by the Clay Cross Hospital Committee. The crowning cremony and the judging of the fancy dress took place in Kennings Park and then the carnival procession perambulated the town. At this carnival Mr G. Collings was elected king, Miss Jessie Marshall, queen, and attendants were Kitty Cook, Vera Stoppard, Joan Ghost and Doreen Smith.

Clay Cross Pom Poms concert party, August 1935. Back row from left to right: Mrs Woodward, Margaret Burgess, Maggie Jones, Violet Broomhall, Linda Hodgkinson, Rene Woodward, Tommy Kilcline. Middle row: Charlie Botham, George Pugh, Wilfred Hall, Marjorie Spencer, Susie Rowan, Rene Williams, Helen Hoggard, Florence Bacon. Front row: Harry Richmond, Joe Hawkins, Alice Worthington, Joan Wedge, Betty Slater, Bobby Lynam, Mrs Gladstone Clark (piano) and Harry Wade (drums).

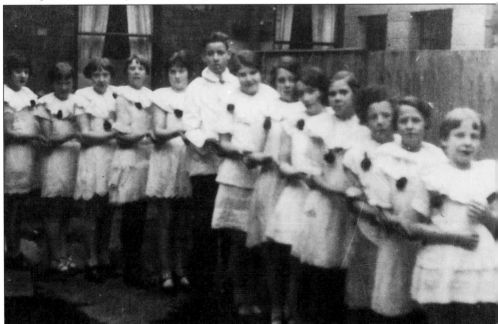

Another photograph of the Clay Cross Pom Poms believed to be around 1929. This particular group entertained at various charity shows with their dance routine throughout the 1930s. In January 1929, they performed for the old people of the Chesterfield Union.

Choosing the Carnival Queen and King.

This photograph was taken at the selection _____ and is reproduced by kind permission of *The Derbyshire Times*, to whom the thanks of the publishers of this programme are given. In addition to the Carnival Queen, King, Attendants, and Maids of Honour, the group includes Judges, Officials, etc.

Royalty for the Clay Cross Carnival, July 1936. Mr Thomas Bellifield was elected king, Vera Stoppard, queen, senior attendants were Jean Hill and Ivy Symonds. Junior attendants were Jean Lee, Ivy Rhodes, Betty Marriott, Jean Barker, Dorothy Marsh and Joan Davis with two tiny tots, June Stevenson and Beryl Binsley.

Vera Stoppard and Thomas Bellifield alighting from an Ashover Light Railway carriage ready for the town procession.

CLAY CROSS CARNIVAL, 1938.

Ballot Form for
The CARNIVAL QUEEN
and Two Attendants.

C	D	A	B	E

Voting Instructions:

Make your selection of the Queen, and insert No. '1' in the space opposite the letter under her photograph. For the Attendants, insert '2' under your second choice, and '3' under your third choice.

You may send in any number of Ballot Forms.

SUBSCRIPTION - - - ONE PENNY.

BALLOT CLOSING DATE, JUNE 2nd, 1938.

Jos. Springs & Sons, General Printers, Clay Cross.

The Carnival Queen and attendants elected by ballot, 1938. Miss Kathleen Staley (D) of Flaxpiece Farm, was elected queen. Her attendants were Miss Joan Davis (C) of Danesmoor and Miss Alice Stone, of Flaxpiece Road. The election was by public ballot; about 5,000 papers were sold and the fund benefitted to the extent of £15. Mr M.H. Boone, Secretary to the Chesterfield Royal Hospital, attended a masked ball at the YMCA at which the winner was announced.

Retiring Queen's Message.

Miss Kathleen Staley.

My Dear Friends,

My term of office has now expired, and I wish my successor a 'Happy and Glorious' Reign.

I take this opportunity to thank all who in any way assisted to make the 1938 Carnival such a success. I hope this year's Carnival produces an even bigger profit.

Yours sincerely,

KATHLEEN STALEY,

1938 Carnival Queen.

Retiring Carnival Queen's message.

The Carnival Queen, 1939.

Miss JOYCE HOBEN.

THE QUEEN'S MESSAGE.

To My Loyal Subjects.

Having, by popular vote, been acclaimed Queen of your Carnival Revels for 1939, I bid you welcome to the merry-makings.

For forty years our Nursing Association and our Hospital Fund Association have done a vast amount of noble work voluntarily, and we desire, through this Carnival, to help them to the utmost of our ability.

'The need is great, the funds are small;
A mite from each means much from all.'

Please do your share to assist in making this year's Carnival an immense financial success.

Carnival Queen 1939.

Miss Joyce Hoben being crowned by Mrs Kenning in Kennings Park. Back row from left to right: Margaret Flavell, Evelyn Mills, Mrs Kenning, George Kenning, Mabel Basely, Joan Ghost. Front row: Margaret Fenner, Carole Flavell, Joyce Hoben, Joan Flavell and Betty Pickering.

Kino Hall, Market Street, was opened on Boxing Day 1909, 'under the most auspicious circumstances'. 'At the matinee performance there was a crowded attendance, while the evening show attracted a capital crowd, the thoroughfare in front of the building being completely blocked, waiting to gain admission fully before the advertised time of commencing, 7.45 pm. Indeed the management was reluctantly compelled to shut the doors at 7.40 and refuse admission to several hundreds of people. If this can be taken as any criterion – and the same state of affairs existed on the following night – then the success of the enterprise is assured'. In 1911 Syd Hopkins was the manager of the Kino and the conductor of the Kino Orchestral Society was Fred Derbyshire.

KINO' HALL,

MARKET STREET,

CLAY CROSS.

NEW UP-TO-DATE
ELECTRIC
THEATRE.

The First Permanent Structure for the purpose in the town.

Grand Opening

On BOXING DAY, DEC. 27. 1909, and Continued during the Week.

Doors Open 7.30.   To Commence 7.45.
Early Doors, 7.15.

Admission at Popular Prices, 3d., 6d., & 1/-
Early Doors. 4d, 8d, 1/3.

SPECIAL MATINEE ON BOXING DAY.
Doors Open 2 p.m., Commence 2.30 p.m.
Prices as above.

CHILDREN'S MATINEE.
Every Saturday at 2.30 p.m., 1d, 2d and 3d.

Only the Finest Series of Animated Pictures will be shown.

ILLUMINATED BY ELECTRICITY.
Upholstered Seats. Heated throughout with Hot Water.

Pianiste & Vocalist - MISS VERE SAULL.

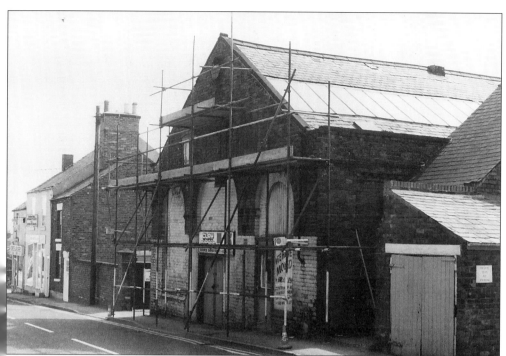

Kino Hall rear entrance in Eyre Street in the process of demolition in 1987. 'The entire work of transforming the Old Market Hall into a first class place of entertainment was done under the personal supervision of the architect Mr Jos Farnsworth, of Clay Cross. The lantern manipulator was Mr P.B. Fonman and Mr Sydney Hopkinson was appointed manager. The management guarantees that the programme shall be absolutely free from vulgarity.'

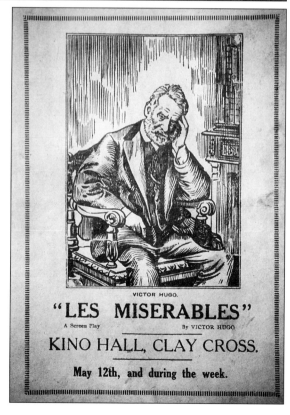

Les Miserables programme.

The Old Picture and Variety Palace was erected on Broadleys and opened on the August bank holiday Monday 1913. 'The stage is of very large dimension and electric light will be generated on the premises by a powerful plant. The bioscope is of the very latest type. Mr Ernest Dakin has charge of the reins and no doubt he will become very popular in Clay Cross'. Mr Bertram Brennan, the eminent pianist and conductor was musical director and 'an efficient orchestra will provide suitable music'.

Palace Theatre,
Clay Cross

Special Attraction.
Week Commencing—
Apr. 27th, 1914.

The Management have great pleasure in announcing their MOST IMPORTANT ENGAGEMENT of **THE**

Venetians.

This Beautiful and highly Artistic 'Act has just concluded a record of 875 Performances in London. Don't miss seeing it.

Times & Prices as usual.

Book your Seats.

Picture Palace postcard for April 1914. The Palace was closed down in June 1926 and in 193 leased to Messrs Burroughs and Watts, who transformed it into a billards hall with eleven table and 'every effort is being made to open for 25th March'. Willie Smith of Graigside, Scarboroug was granted the billiard license.

The Clay Cross Hippodrome Ltd was established in 1922. Construction of the Hippodrome, situated opposite the Palace on the Broadleys, commenced in April 1924 and was opened on 12 April 1925 when 'crowded houses have been the rule every evening this week'. The managing director was Mr Herbert Minney, Clay Cross, and his two co-directors were Jesse Williams of Stonebroom and George H. Yates of Leeds.

On Monday 19 February 1940, the Hippodrome was gutted by a fire. 'It was not long before the roof fell in with a resounding crash. This sent the flames even higher, and streets in the vicinity, which were quiet... quickly became alive with people. A large crowd saw the balcony cave in. The pace at which the fire wrought its havoc was almost incredible'. On the night of the fire Mr Dick Minney was the resident manager and lived in a house at the rear of the cinema.

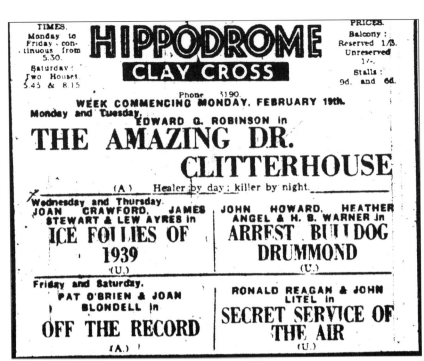

HIPPODROME
CLAY CROSS

WEEK COMMENCING MONDAY, FEBRUARY 19th.

Monday and Tuesday.
EDWARD G. ROBINSON in

THE AMAZING DR. CLITTERHOUSE

(A)   Healer by day : killer by night.

Wednesday and Thursday.

JOAN CRAWFORD, JAMES STEWART & LEW AYRES in

ICE FOLLIES OF 1939
(U.)

JOHN HOWARD, HEATHER ANGEL & H. B. WARNER in

ARREST BULLDOG DRUMMOND
(U.)

Friday and Saturday.

PAT O'BRIEN & JOAN BLONDELL in

OFF THE RECORD
(A.)

RONALD REAGAN & JOHN LITEL in

SECRET SERVICE OF THE AIR
(U.)

The last film to be shown at the Clay Cross Hippodrome.

HIPPODROME
CLAY CROSS

OWING TO THE DISASTROUS FIRE WE CANNOT OFFER OUR PATRONS THEIR USUAL ENTERTAINMENT. HOWEVER, WE HOPE THAT ERE LONG WE CAN PROVIDE ANOTHER CINEMA TO WELCOME YOU WITH THE SAME HIGH STANDARD OF PROGRAMMES TOGETHER WITH THE COMFORTS YOU HAD SO OFTEN ENJOYED.

HARRY MIDDLETON,
Director and Secretary.

In the same week of the fire this notice appeared in the *Derbyshire Times* on 23 January 194_
and initiated a long and complex struggle to get the cinema rebuilt. The Board of Trad_
supported the scheme but only when housing and labour needs would permit. The UD_
reopened the case for a cinema in 1952 and the following year a building licence for £5,000 w_
granted, but considered totally inadequate - the cinema was never rebuilt.

PUBLIC HALL, CLAY CROSS.
ON SATURDAY, OCTOBER 11th, 1862.

AFRICAN MINSTRELS,

From the St. James's Hall, London, and the Crystal Palace Sydenham, will have the honour to present their

REFINED NEGRO ENTERTAINMENT!!

on each of the above evenings, consisting of Ballads, Part-Songs, and Vocal, Instrumental and Terpsichorean Extravaganzas.

PROGRAMME :—PART FIRST.

Opening Chorus	Company
Beautiful Star	Mr Barrett
Peter Gray	Mr T. H. Raynor
The Stolen Child	Mr Gambia
Ring the Banjo	Mr Southern
Let Me Kiss him for his Mother	Mr Barrett
Ladies wont you Marry	Mr T. H. Raynor
Rosa Lee	Mr Gambia
A Little more Cider	Mr Southern
Thou art so Near	Mr Barrett
Willie has gone for a Soldier	Mr T. H. Raynor

(An Interval of Ten minutes)

PART SECOND.—Varieties.

Operatic Solo (ala Signora Screechini)	Mr Southern
Old Bob Ridley	Mr T. H. Raynor
Silver Belt Jig	Mr Redman

———

THE HAUNTED HOUSE!

The Tenant	Mr Gambia
The Ghost	Mr Southern

———

Parliamentary Discussion	Mr T. H. Raynor

(Or any other Man!)

Ballad	Mr Barrett

———

THE MUSIC LESSON ; OR, TALENT AND STUPIDITY !

The Master—Mr Gambia.   The Pupils—Mr Raynor and Mr Redman.

Who will Introduce a Violin Extravaganza.

Concluding with the New Nigger Break down—

JOHNNY ROACH.

Doors open at Half-past Seven, Commence at Eight, and Conclude at Ten.

Reserved Seats, 2s. Unreserved Seats, 1s. Back Seats, 6d

African Minstrels, October 1862.

97

The 1963 Whit Walk procession approaching the Red Shield (Triangle Club) situated on the left. This club was opened by the Duchess of Portland in February 1921. The building was a YMCA hut brought from Clipstone camp and 'It is said to be the largest of its kind in the country'. The hall could accommodate about 500 people, could be used for whist drives, dances and other social functions and included four billiard tables, a committee room, an office and a bathroom.

Miss Holdsworth

CLAY CROSS BROTHERHOOD RED TRIANGLE INSTITUTE.

Mr. HARRY N. HOLMES
O.B.E., F.R.G.S., WILL DELIVER HIS

ILLUSTRATED TRAVELOGUE

"THE GRAND CANYON
AND

PETRIFIED FOREST OF ARIZONA,"

IN THE CONCERT HALL, ON
SATURDAY, OCTOBER 29th, 1921, at 7-30 p.m.

SOLOIST:

Mr. JOSEPH LYCETT (SHEFFIELD)

ADMISSION PROGRAMME:
Reserved Seat C.14. Two Shillings.

Reservation ticket for Miss Holdsworth of Alma House.

A note on the back of this postcard records 'Baby Welcome', Clay Cross Hall, July 1918. In November 1918, the Clay Cross UDC resolved to join the county maternity and child welfare scheme. In the *Derbyshire Times*, December 1920, there is reference to Baby's Welcome headquarters at the parochial schools. This Baby Welcome was arranged by Miss Clarkson, the health visitor, assisted by Mrs Steen, Miss Willets (county secretary), Mrs Reed and Mesdames Blake, Drew, Elliott, T.G. Griffin, Keeling, Marsh, Spriggs, Sparrow, S. Smith, Smalley, Taylor and Mrs Jackson, of Clay Cross Hall.

Clay Cross Baby Show, September 1870.

CLAY CROSS.——BABY SHOW.——An amusing exhibition took place at Mr. E. V. Pearson's auction establishment on Friday evening last. Notice was given that a baby show would be held on that night, and a very large crowd of people from Clay Cross and that vicinity assembled to witness the exhibition. Eighteen mothers entered their last-born as candidates for the prize, which was a valuable set of trays, given by Mr. Pearson. The conditions was that the heaviest baby under 12 months old should be the winner. Two person were chosen from the vast concourse of people to weigh the respective candidates, whose account shows the following result :— Colledge, 28¼lbs. ; W. H. Howitt, 25¾lbs. ; Edward Barsby, 22¼lbs.; Francis Garton, 21¾lbs.; Alice Stanley, 21¾lbs.; G. S. Lane, 21¾lbs.; George Evans, 21¼lbs.; Richard Wharton, 21¼lbs.; W. Oldbury, 20¾lbs.; J. Morrell, 19½lbs. M. Wilde, 19¼lbs.; Peter Scott, 18¾lbs.; E. Walker, 18lbs.; Polly Marsden, 17¾lbs.; Sarah Ann Whyman, 17¾lbs.; and Harriet Robinson, 16lbs. Mr. Pearson presented each of the unsuccessful candidates with a useful bread knife. The whole of the candidates were neatly and cleanly dressed ; and as a matter of fact, each mother's child looked the prettiest.
LONGSTONE

An outing for the poor children of Clay Cross organised by the Motor Cycle and Light Car Club, July 1925. Over 500 children were conveyed in a fleet of thirty-seven vehicles consisting of motor coaches, lorries and cars. 'Prior to the start the Clay Cross Fairground presented an animated scene and a large crowd assembled to see the cars off. The convoy proceeded to Higham, Ambergate, Matlock, Darley Dale, Rowsley, Chatsworth Park, Baslow and back home through Chesterfield. Stops were made at Ambergate and in Chatsworth Park. The following loaned their vehicles for the occasion: Sir E. Shental, Brig Gen Jackson, George Kenning (4), J. Rorrison, J. Turvey, W. Stoppard, Mr J. Lester, J.H. White, W. Francis, F. Spencer, J. Flavell, H. Rowbotham, A. Cutts, H. Clark, J. Hudson, L. Jayne, M. Marriott, L. Callidine, Mr Gallagher and the Chesterfield Co-op Society. The following acted as route marshalls: C.H. Bloor, W. Cutts, W. Whiston, L. Spriggs and A. Harold. The Clay Cross and District Motor Cycle and Light Car Club was established in April 1924, with its headquarters at Rowbotham's garage, Chesterfield Road. The annual subscription was 5s.

Kenning's trip to Skegness in 1935, when some 360 OAPs and elderly widows enjoyed a day out at the YMCA holiday home. Front row from left to right: Abraham Street, George Griffin, Mrs Kenning, John Hopkin, George Kenning, Mr Coupe, Mr Wills and J. Callidine. Mrs Wilkes and back row: Albert Winsbury (general secretary of the YMCA), T.W. Palfreyman, John Elton, Mrs Bullimore, Mrs Holbrook, Mrs Wright, Mr Yeomans, William Quemby, Frank Tuckley (chairman of the YMCA).

The Outing Club at the Crown Inn, Clay Cross, established around 1895. Prior to the introduction of the internal combustion engine the members were transported on these excursions by horse drawn waggonettes. In May 1907, the *Clay Cross Chronicle* reported that 'A party numbering about twenty chartered a motor car and had a tour around Loughboro, Leicestershire and Nottinghamshire'. The following June, 'The party chartered a motor-char-a-banc and had a splendid drive to the Dukeries'.

Sanger's Circus parading down the High Street, October 1903.

SANGER'S CIRCUS.—Sanger's circus visited Clay Cross on Monday last, and considering the inclement weather and the fact that Buffalo Bill's Wild West Show had been in Chesterfield the previous Friday, the performances were well patronised. The outstanding features of the exhibition were an acrobatic musical act by the Ventos, a trapeze performance by E herdo and Pugh, and Burton's troupe of canine wonders, introducing the high diving dog "Blondin." The musicians, who were violinists, played their instruments in almost every conceivable position, and concluded with a dance by the ladies, for which they provided their own music. The trapeze performance evoked well-merited applause, many feats being safely accomplished, the most daring being a dive through a hoop from the top of the tent into the net. Endless amusement was caused by the acrobatic clowns, who attempted the feats of the previous performers. The dogs went through some clever tricks, and were remarkably good at high jumping, whilst the high diving dog after climbing a ladder to the top of the tent, dived into a blanket held in the ring by four men. The other usual attractions of a circus including juggling, riding, push ball, football and boxing matches between elephants and clowns, were amusing, whilst the patter of the latter caused endless amusement. On the whole the performance was a good one, and was much appreciated. As a special attraction to the public a prize of a suite of furniture was offered by the circus promoters to the seat-holder who obtained the "lucky" ticket. The suite was purchased from the establishment of Messrs. T. Greaves and Co., Complete House Furnishers, and has been on view in their windows in Market-street during the past few days. The "lucky" number was drawn from the hat by a Church Brigade lad, and the holder of the corresponding number proved to be a Mr. Cocking, of Hilly Fields, North Wingfield. Mr. Cocking certainly has reasons to remember his visit to the circus with pleasure.

Tassy Smith, Waterloo Street, proudly displaying his prize celery. In 1841 the CXC were instrumental in setting up a Cottage Garden Society, the main objectives of which were 'to promote the cultivation of gardens useful and ornamental, to encourage habits of industry and domestic taste and to foster a love for home amongst the working class'. In 1852, the society was renamed the Clay Cross Floral and Horticultural Society and its annual show attracted thousands of vistors.

Eliza Stocks, one of the world's 'greatest grandmothers' who reared twelve of her own children in the 'Monkey Hollow' (Waterloo Street) and also took in a foundling that was left in the yard. Despite the stern appearance, Eliza was a caring and gentle person with a heart 'as big as a frying-pan' and always willing to give her neighbours a hand. She lived in the 'Monkey Hollow' all her life and died at the age of 77 in November 1936.

The Vallence Band local entertainers outside the George and Dragon, c. 1890, taken by the landlord Joseph Buxton. The town had a good number of visiting entertainers from the 1850s and the 1891 returns record George Brough, musical hall act, residing in Froggatt's Row as a boarder.

Seven
The Company

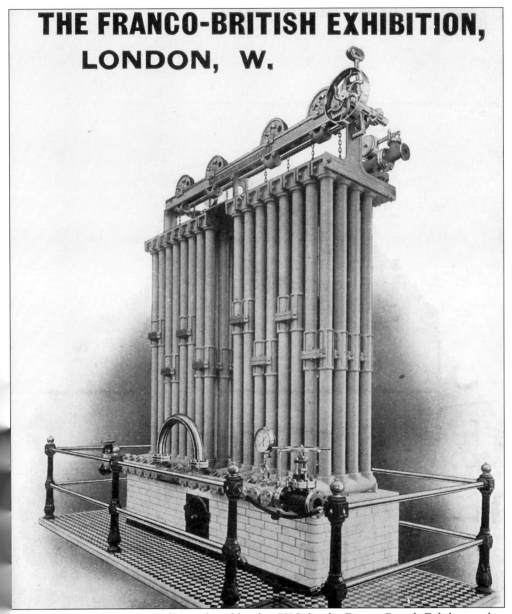

THE FRANCO-BRITISH EXHIBITION, LONDON, W.

This rare postcard was especially produced by the CXC for the Franco-British Exhibition that took place in September 1908, when the company were awarded two gold medals for their economisers and coal products. This was the first postcard to successfully advertise their products.

These CXC Gold Medal postcards were inaugurated after the Franco-British Exhibition to advertise their coal products and particularly in London, where much of their house coal was sold. There were three series of cards distributed; each set contained twenty-five cards and many of the same postcards were used in the different sets but in a varying order, with new ones occasionally added.

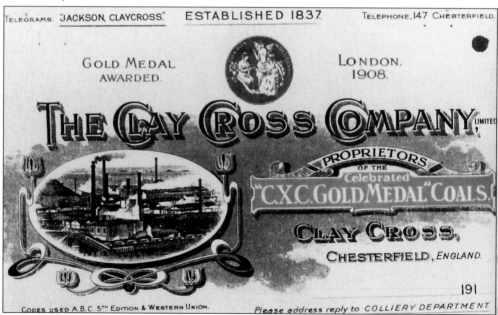

This letter head also celebrates the CXC Gold Medal Coal. Albert Heath, a photographer based in Thanet Street, took many of the company's photographs that depicted their coal being conveyed from the coalface, screened and dispatched. The full set of Gold Medal Cards illustrates and preserves for prosperity an industry and community that has now sadly disappeared.

No. 102.] **300 YARDS BELOW GROUND.** [See No. 111.
Two typical Colliers winning their bread getting the
celebrated "C.X.C. Gold Medal" Coal.

The caption for this particular scene appears innocuous enough but scratch beneath the surface and a different story is revealed. When this photograph was taken around 1910, it was illegal to fill the tubs with a shovel and anyone caught doing so would be sacked. Before the company would amend this rule they demanded that the men accept a reduction of 5d per ton on the basic rate. The company expected the men to fill the coal by hand, forks or riddles so the slack (small coal) could be left underground.

No. 119.] **GOING UP.** [See No. 111.
"Tubs" of the celebrated "C.X.C. Gold Medal"
Coal arriving at the Pit bottom ready for hauling up
the shaft to the surface.

'Running' on at the Clay Cross No. 2 Pit Bottom – note the large lumps of coal in the tubs. Concomitant with riddling coal was the pernicious practice of confiscating a full tub of coal to the advantage of the owners if as little as 5 lb of 'dirt' was found in any tub. This practice was widespread and the miners had no avenue for redress until the advent of the check-weighman who would negotiate with the company weighman as to the acceptability of a particular tub.

No. 116.]   [See No. 104.

ARRIVAL OF COAL AT PIT SHAFT.
"C.X.C. Gold Medal" Coal arriving at the bottom
of the shaft ready for hauling to the surface 300
yards above.

At one time, at most of the Derbyshire collieries, the miners had to get 120 lb or more to the cwt and as much as 29 cwt to the ton. This was known as the 'long weight' system and remained in practice until 1873, when the Mines Regulation Act became fully operative and was substituted by the imperial ton; the use of weights, instead of the measure, was also introduced.

The CXC had four rescue teams that were all trained at the Mansfield Woodhouse Rescue Station. A member of the gaffers association in 1908, commented, 'Looking over the past history of the Midland coalfield he imagined that rescue apparatus might perhaps save one life in twenty years, and the cost of saving it would, he supposed, work out at anything from £10,000 to £20,000. Surely £20,000 could be made of greater service to mankind than that!'

No. 107.] **DOWN A COAL MINE.**
Blacksmith performing his daily duties in the stables in one of the Pits producing the renowned "C.X.C. Gold Medal" Coal.

A blacksmith and his striker shoeing a pony in the No. 2 Pit stables. At one time the company had nearly 300 pit ponies working underground – one of the main reasons why the company established its several farms to provide fodder. Many pit blacksmiths were frequently criticised by farriers for having little knowledge about the shoeing of ponies and their lack of 'horse knowledge'.

The CXC's No. 2 Pit prior to closure with the headstocks at the centre of the picture. In December 1933, preparations were being made for the closure of this pit at the end of April 1934, at a cost of £1,000. The closure was estimated to save about £15,000 per annum. The pit ceased production on Saturday 12 May 1934 and the dismantling of the surface plant commenced in July.

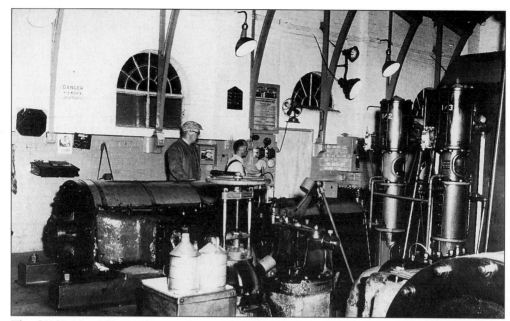

The CXC's No. 5 Pit winding engine at Morton, installed in 1865, designed by William Howe and manufactured and erected by A. Handyside & Co., Derby. The engine was 200 hp with a stroke of 5 ft and a bore of 30 ins. The winding drum was 15 ft in diameter and the pit 305 yards deep. The weight of coal drawn up at any one time was 40 cwt, raised in 35 seconds at a rate of 1,568 ft per minute.

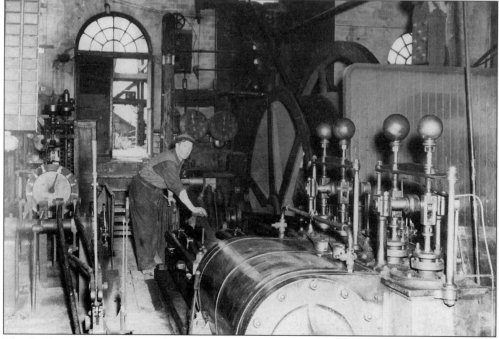

The CXC's No. 2 winding engine prior to demolition, with Mr B. Hooper giving the engine a polish. Although the pit closed in 1934, it continued to be used as an escape shaft from Parkhouse No. 7 Pit.

No. 7 Parkhouse Pit winding engine – unfortunately the builders of this engine remain elusive so the author would be grateful for any information about it. This particular CXC colliery was known locally as 'Catty' Pit, supposedly so-called after one of the sinkers had consumed a cat pie at his lodgings. This pit was sunk through the foundations of Park Hall, the Deincourt's manor house.

The Parkhouse Pit-head baths and canteen were officially opened on 16 September 1939, by Brigadier General G.M. Jackson, MD of the CXC and chairman of the Derbyshire District Miners Welfare Central Council. Bath accomodation was provided for 768 men, with 51 shower baths and a canteen at a total cost of £13,000. The workmens' subscriptions amounted to 6d each per week. The CXC leased the site for 99 years at an annual rent of 1s and provided the electricity, steam, bathing and swilling water free.

Changing the wheel and rope during the Easter break of 1929 at 'Catty' Pit. This job was performed periodically because of constant wear and tear; it was not an easy job and required about fourteen men. A pole of strong timber, firmly secured with rope stays, was erected in a vertical position and with the aid of block and tackle apparatus, the old wheel was removed and replaced by the new one.

The team of workers that changed the wheel and rope, Easter 1929. To date only three people can be identified; back row, far left: Raymond Carlin. Back row, far right: Cocky Roberts. Middle row, seated far right: Bert Slater.

No. 120.]   **A TYPICAL PIT PONY.**   [See No. 124.
The day of ill-treatment of pit ponies is rapidly passing away. At the Clay Cross Collieries, where the celebrated "C.X.C. Gold Medal" Coal is worked, the ponies—the illustration is a typical example—are well cared for and receive very humane treatment. The bridle worn by the pony was adopted to protect the animal's eyes and head in places where there is a danger of its coming into contact with the low roof.

Here the CXC's caption begins with 'The day of ill treatment of pit ponies is rapidly passing away'. The unvarnished truth reveals that the colliery manager was fined £20 for allowing four horses to be worked in an unfit condition and for allowing ponies to work on roads not large enough for them to pass through. All five ostlers were fined £3 each as well as costs for similar offences, and two of them were fined for not keeping a daily record of ponies under their care.

No. 113.]   **OFF UP.**   [See No. 122.
Colliers—getters of the "C.X.C. Gold Medal" Coal—being hauled from bottom of shaft to surface 300 yards above.

Walter Symonds, onsetter at the CXC's No. 2 Pit, about to send the men up the shaft after completing their stint at the coal face. This particular cage was a single decked, flat topped cage and was guided up the shaft by shoes fitted to the top and bottom of the cage. The young lad on the right of the picture is thirteen year old Richard Edward Mullis. In 1911, an Act of Parliament raised the age at which boys could work underground to fourteen.

Three miners at the CXC No. 2 Pit repairing a subsidiary road. Sometimes miners had to work beyond their strength in an attempt to make a living wage and, when working in 'abnormal conditions', they relied on the generosity of the management for 'make up' pay. This generally fell far short of what was considered to be a fair return for a good day's work and caused much ill feeling when the seam hit a fault.

A group of colliers and a young lad on their way to the pit bottom at 'knock off'. Note the soft flat caps that these workers are wearing. In 1910, the ponies 'pit cap' was introduced, 'Constructed from a single piece of leather, it is extremely light, ventilation is secured by perforation, the projections serve as blinkers and the animals suffer not the slightest inconveniance'. Pit helmets did not come into general use until after Nationalisation.

A view of No. 6 Morton Colliery struck by lightning, 3 August 1879.

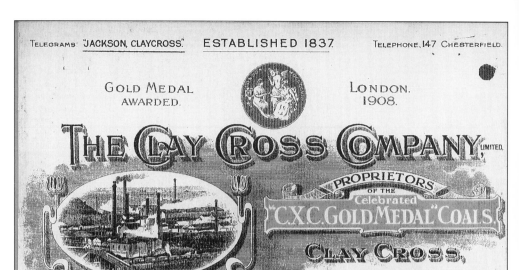

TELEGRAMS: "JACKSON, CLAYCROSS." **ESTABLISHED 1837** TELEPHONE, 147 CHESTERFIELD.

GOLD MEDAL
AWARDED.

LONDON.
1908.

THE CLAY CROSS COMPANY, LIMITED,

PROPRIETORS OF THE Celebrated "C.X.C. GOLD MEDAL" COALS.

CLAY CROSS,
CHESTERFIELD, ENGLAND.

191

CODES USED A.B.C. 5TH EDITION & WESTERN UNION.

Please address reply to COLLIERY DEPARTMENT.

CONTRACTORS TO H.M. GOVERNMENT.

ALL OFFERS SUBJECT TO OUR USUAL CLAUSES AS TO STRIKES, LOCKOUTS, & ACCIDENTS, INCIDENCE OF FUTURE DUES, CHARGES, & RAILWAY RATES.

PRICE LIST.

TERMS.—Nett Cash on the 14th of the month following delivery.   These prices are subject to alteration without notice.

	Per ton of 2,240 lbs. at pit.		Per ton of 2,240 lbs. at pit.
Best Main—The best Coal produced in Derbyshire		**Large House Nuts**—Through 3-inch and over 2-inch screen	
Best Main Cubes—Through 5-inch and over 2½-inch screen		**Hand-Picked Deep**—An ideal coal for Farmers	
Large Main Nuts—Through 2½-inch and over 1½-inch screen		**Hand-Picked Cobbles**—A first-class kitchen coal	
Hasland Brights—Through 8-inch and over 4½-inch screen		**Treble-Screened Cobbles**— Through 5½-inch and over 3-inch screen. A splendid all-round coal.	
Best Derbys—Through 10-inch and over 5-inch screen		**Cobbles**—A very useful coal	
Derby Cubes—Through 5-inch and over 3-inch screen .:.		**Deep Hard Nuts**—Through 3-inch and over 1½-inch screen. A first-rate hard nut.	
Derby Large Nuts—Through 4½-inch and over 2-inch screen		**Hand-Picked Hards**—A first-rate steam coal ..	
Best House—Over 2½-inch screen .. .. A superior coal suitable for all household purposes.		**Best Loco**	

A Clay Cross Company lamp check. It was the responsibility of the banksman to search miners for contraband before they descended into the pit. He also collected these lamp checks which were sent to the pit bottom and displayed on a board to check who was still in the pit. At the end of the shift these were then returned to the lamp room. This system appears to have been introduced at Clay Cross soon after the Parkhouse Pit explosion in 1882.

A couple of deputies doing their safety rounds, checking the roof and seeing that the haulage rope is well lubricated. Regulations to ensure that only competent persons should be employed as deputies, examiners and shotfirers came into force in 1911, and they had to be able to test for gas and measure the air current, besides having the necessary coal mining experience to do the work properly.

The banksman had complete charge of the pit cage when the miners were ascending and descending the shaft. During winding operations he communicated with the onsetter at the pit bottom and the winder by a series of raps on the signals. The banksman and the onsetter had a very responsible and trustworthy job, but they were relatively low paid workers.

The CXC's women brickworkers, December 1919. At this date the company were fined for contravening the Factories and Workshops Act by employing five women on night work at their Old Tupton brickworks. The five women involved were Martha Jemima Ward, Martha Young, Violet Whitting, Emma Rowan and Hannah Bradshaw. According to the HMI, the employment of women after 8.00 pm had not been allowed for the past half-century and following a report to the Home Office in November, Hannah Bradshaw met with a serious accident at 2.00 am. The company were fined 40s in each case plus witness costs. During the First World War, the CXC were short of labour with so many of their workers accepting the King's shilling – including three of General Jackson's sons – and they recruited women workers for the screens and 'Bomb Shop'. In January 1919, it was reported that Jessie Roe, a munitions worker, of 208 Furnace Hill, Clay Cross, had fractured her thigh at the Clay Cross Workers and was conveyed to the Chesterfield Hospital.

This postcard of the CXC furnaces was posted at Eastwood on 29 January 1910, and shows the 'Big Wall', the only one of its kind still extant in the East Midlands. However proposals are being made to demolish it and the Department of Environment are not prepared to list it. This postcard is quite rare and depicts a train of empty 'Clay cxc Cross' waggons being drawn from the works.

A group of foundry workers, c. 1915, with Fredrick Cresswell, foundry manager, seated on the far right of the front row. Fredrick Cresswell was employed with the CXC for some sixty-seven years, retiring in 1929 at the age of 75. He was born in Clay Cross in 1854 and was bound as an apprentice in 1871 to 'the art of Moulding' to Sir William Jackson and Sir Joshua Walmsley.

A view from inside the works showing the two cooling towers and a mountain of slag behind the 'cracker'. In May 1921, part of this slag heap collapsed and buried alive Mrs May Dunstanley Milner. It took about six hours to recover the body and the impact had totally crushed her and severed her left hand. This slag heap was locally called the Cinder Tip and was about 100 feet high. Mrs Dunstanley had four children and lived with her elderly mother on the fairground.

CXC managers, foremen and office staff, c. 1917. Standing on the far left with hand on hip is Fredrick Cresswell, foundry foreman, and sitting in the front row on the far left is George Bramley, foundry manager. George worked for the CXC for sixty years and worked his way up to foundry manager and then engineer. On his marriage he lived in Park Terrace, then Eldon House and finally at North End House on Chesterfield Road. He died in March 1921, at the age of 78 and is buried in the family grave in Clay Cross Church.

Coney Green Farm, c. 1910. This farm was managed by James Muirhead (snr) who came from Scotland to Clay Cross to manage the CXC's farms. He met with a tragic accident in 1881 and was killed when he was thrown from his horse. In 1905/6 his son James was appointed farm bailiff and introduced double-farrow ploughing and motor ploughing to the district. He was a member of the Clay Cross District Ploughing Association and treasurer to the Clay Cross and Alfreton Heavy Horse Society.

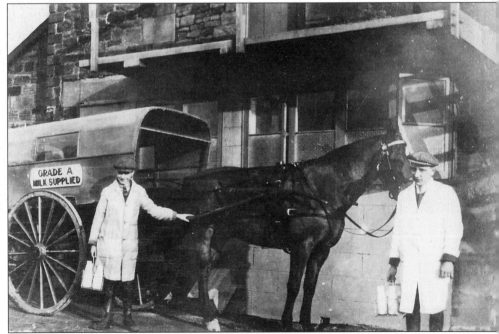

Coney Green Farm dairy, built in January 1910. Before being appointed to the farm bailiff's job James Muirhead (jnr) was senior ostler and had charge of the CXC's 313 pit ponies and horses and thirty working horses on the farms and pit-bank. At this date Muirhead had responsibilty for the cultivation of some 230 acres of land for hay, oats, turnips, mangels and potatoes – all with the exception of the potatoes were used to feed the pit ponies.

Eight
Trade Unions
and Politics

The banner on the right-hand side of the photograph is the Clay Cross Lodge banner inaugurated in July 1874, under the auspices of the South Yorkshire Miners Association – 'On Monday the miners of the Clay Cross district paraded through the town head by the Clay Cross 7th Volunteer Band. The demonstration was in honour of the inauguration of the new banner or the district. The banner, without exception, is the finest piece of workmanship of its kind in this part of the county. On one side is the collier and his family before the Union and the collier nd his wife after the Union, whilst on the reverse side is painted in a beautiful style 'The Unmerciful Servant' over which hangs part of a figure of a female with the motto 'Let Truth nd Love Prevail". The banner was made by Elam of Bethnal Green, London, at a cost of £60. After parading the town, the men with their wives and sweethearts, sat down for tea in the New Market Hall, which was filled twice to excess, nearly 800 partaking of the 'cup of cheers but not nebriates'. An SYMA lodge was established at the Parkhouse Hotel, Danesmoor, in November, 375.

The Derbyshire Miners Association, Danesmoor Lodge banner, displayed in the back yard of their old headquarters at the Parkhouse Hotel, with the late Derek Wilde, the landlord, looking on. The motto in the centre reads 'We Unite To Assist Each Other'. The title of the other banner behind Derek simply reads 'Derbyshire Miners Association 1880' – the year when the DMA was established; 'Great was the rejoicing when the men marched up to the Angel Hotel, Clay Cross, and the new Union was fairly launched'.

Coal picking on the No. 1 Pit tip during the 1893, Great Lock Out. This national lock-out caused severe hardship and much suffering and the Clay Cross Allotment Society relieved much hunger with the provision of vegetables and the like. Amongst the principal subscribers to the Clay Cross Relief Fund were the *Sun Newspaper*, £47; CX Co-op, £21; *London Daily Chronicle*, £20; *Derby Co-op*, £10 and a good number of shopkeepers provided soup and food.

A group of Parkhouse miners outside the 'Bottom Pub' after a lodge meeting of the DMA, *c.* 1903. All the CXC's pits with the exception of their Morton No. 5 Pit, were 'house coal' pits and many miners were laid off work during most summers when there was little demand for house coal. A school teacher in 1905 said, 'Children often come to school without any meals, but when questioned they are too proud to say they have not had any'.

'Heath Robinson' device erected over the Press Brook at Holmgate to transport 'outcrop' coal across the brook during the 1926 strike. The coal is very close to the surface in this area and there is evidence of it being mined in the sixteenth century. Thomas Holdsworth was mining coal here at the Alma Colliery from about 1850, and New Market Colliery was very close by.

CLAY CROSS

Urban District Council Election,

THURSDAY, JULY 3rd, 1919.

LADIES AND GENTLEMEN,

Nominated as a Representative of the Clay Cross Labour Party, which is a Branch of the Federated Trades Union Party, I, the undersigned, offer myself for election at the forthcoming contest for the Urban District Council.

I am in favour of a progressive policy, including the provision of adequate storage for our water supply and the repair of the roads with more durable and cleanly material such as granite.

The Housing Scheme will be strongly supported by me, and as far as possible so will the erection of w.c's. to existing workmen's dwellings where it is convenient.

In view of the Rent Restrictions Bill coming into operation, which will compel landlords when giving notice of the increase in rent to inform the tenant of his right to appeal to the sanitary authority on the question of the habitable qualities of the house, I hope it will enable me to assist in seeing that workmen's dwellings are put into a proper state of repair, and that the filthy backyards, oft-times ankle deep in sludge, are put into a more respectable condition to enable our women and children to move in decency.

I am in favour of the Extension of the Boundary so as to bring into this ratepaying area the Clay Cross Company's Works, and remove the anomaly of the greatest users of our streets for their commodity paying their rates into other areas.

I am in favour of giving publicity to all matters of public interest, using at the same time my best endeavour for strict economy without sacrificing the health and comfort of the community.

Working Women ! Take advantage of the new Franchise Act and Vote !

Working Men ! Remember you must take a hand in Reconstruction.

I remain, yours faithfully,

J. RENSHAW.

The Polling Booth will be open at Clay Cross and Danesmoor, from 12 to 8 p.m.

VOTE LABOUR.

The Bottom Name on Ballot Paper.

Printed and Published by J. W. Petts, High Street, Clay Cross.

n Renshaw, attired in the chain of office of the General President of the Sheffield Equalised
dependent Order of Druids, a post which he held for two years in 1933 and 1934; he was also
asurer of the local Shakespeare Lodge for twenty-two years. He commenced work at the age
10, picking ironstone for Mark Armstrong, and two years later became a pony driver in
C's No. 2 Pit. When 17, he worked in a stall with Benjamin Cook, who was the treasurer of
ay Cross No. 1 Branch DMA, of which he became an active member. He was the first
retary to the Clay Cross Labour Party, president of the Parkhouse Miners Branch and an
cted member of the Clay Cross UDC. He earned the sobriquet 'the stormy petrel' and took
the cudgels on behalf of all and sundry who appealed to him for support. John Renshaw died
16 December 1936, and was buried in Clay Cross Cemetery.

Samuel Wright Rowarth, 'the esteemed general secretary of the Nottinghamshire ar Derbyshire Enginemen's and Firemen's Union'. This portrait was presented to him in Ap 1918, together with an illuminated address and a purse of gold for twenty-six years service to th Union. Mr Rowarth was born at Bamford in 1847 and migrated to Openshaw in Manchest with his parents. At the age of 6 he came to Clay Cross where he attended the 'Stable Schoo He started work as a 'bat-picker' at CXC's No. 3 Pit at the age of 10, working 12 hours per da He joined the Clay Cross Volunteer Band in 1863 and played the second cornet when they wo first prize at Belle Vue in September 1867. He was winder over the sinkers at Parkhouse P (1867), Clifton Colliery, Notts. (1868) and Pilsley Colliery (1870). In 1872 he joined th Chesterfield Enginemen's Sick Club and eventually set up a branch at the Furnace Inn, Cl Cross. This society was not a registered society and, together with forty-six other members, the decided to become legal and established the Enginemen's and Firemen's Union at the Furna Inn, Clay Cross, on 22 February 1892. In 1911 he left Clay Cross to take up residence at th Union's new offices in Mansfield and retired in 1918. He died at Beech Avenue, Mansfield, February 1924.